## DATE DUE

| | |
|---|---|
| SEP 30 1992 | |
| APR 1 7 2003 | |
| DEC 1 2 2003 | |
| MAY 0 2 2018 | |
| | |
| | |
| | |
| | |
| | |
| | |
| | |
| | |
| | |
| | |
| | |
| | |
| | |
| | |

|

# JOHN STEINBECK

## Literature and Life Series
[Formerly Modern Literature
and World Dramatists]

Selected list of titles:

Complete list of titles in the series available from publisher on
request.

# JOHN STEINBECK

*Paul McCarthy*

FREDERICK UNGAR PUBLISHING CO.
NEW YORK

Copyright © 1980 by Frederick Ungar Publishing Co., Inc.
*Printed in the United States of America*
*Design by Anita Duncan*


Library of Congress Cataloging in Publication Data

McCarthy, Paul, 1921–
    John Steinbeck.

    (Modern literature monographs)
    Bibliography: p.
    Includes index.
    1.   Steinbeck, John, 1902–1968—Criticism and
interpretation.
PS3537.T3234Z723      813'.5'2      78–20929
    ISBN 0-8044-2606-6 (cloth)
    ISBN 0-8044-6461-8 (pbk.)

*First paperback edition, 1984*

*For Phyllis*

# Contents

# Chronology

1902  John Ernest Steinbeck is born 27 February, in Salinas, California.

1919  Graduates from Salinas High School.

1920  Drops out of Stanford for months of varied work.

1923  Returns to Stanford as English major.

1924  Two stories appear in *The Stanford Spectator*.

1925  Leaves Stanford without degree. Works briefly as a reporter and as a construction worker in New York City.

1926  Returns to California.

1929  *Cup of Gold* is published.

1930  Marries Carol Henning and lives in Pacific Grove. Meets Ed Ricketts.

1932  *The Pastures of Heaven* is published. Moves to Los Angeles.

1933  Returns to Pacific Grove. *To a God Unknown* is published. First two parts of *The Red Pony* are published.

1934  Steinbeck's mother dies. "The Murder" is selected as an O. Henry Prize story.

1935  *Tortilla Flat* is published. Steinbeck gains national fame.

1936  *In Dubious Battle* is published. Moves to Los Gatos. Steinbeck's father dies. Travels to Mexico.

1937  *Of Mice and Men* is published. In New York and
      Pennsylvania, works on stage version which wins
      Drama Critics' Circle Award. *The Red Pony* in three
      parts is published. Makes first trip to Europe.

1938  *The Long Valley* and "Their Blood Is Strong" are
      published.

1939  *The Grapes of Wrath* is published.

1940  Wins the Pulitzer Prize for *The Grapes of Wrath*. Ex-
      plores the Gulf of California with Ed Ricketts.

1941  *Sea of Cortez* appears.

1942  Is divorced from Carol Henning. *The Moon Is Down*
      is published. Writes *Bombs Away* for the U.S. Air
      Force.

1943  Marries Gwyndolen Conger (Gwen Verdon). Covers
      the war in Europe for the *New York Herald Tribune*.

1944  Son Thomas is born. *Cannery Row*, dated 1945, is
      published in December.

1945  *The Red Pony* in four parts is published. "The Pearl
      of the World" appears in *Woman's Home Com-
      panion*. Begins permanent residence in New York
      City.

1946  Son John is born.

1947  Travels to Russia with photographer Robert Capa.
      *The Wayward Bus* and *The Pearl* are published.

1948  Is divorced from Gwyndolen Conger. Ed Ricketts dies.
      *A Russian Journal* is published. Is elected to Amer-
      ican Academy of Arts and Letters.

1950  Marries Elaine Scott. *Burning Bright* is published.

1951  *The Log from the Sea of Cortez* is published; includes
      "About Ed Ricketts."

1952  *East of Eden* is published.

1954  *Sweet Thursday* is published.

1957  *The Short Reign of Pippin IV* is published.

1958  *Once There Was a War* is published.

1960  Takes three-months' tour of America with dog Charley.

1961  *The Winter of Our Discontent* is published. Is his-
      torian for Project Mohole off Mexican coast.

1962   *Travels with Charley in Search of America* is pub-
       lished. Receives the Nobel Prize for literature.

1963   Tours Europe for U.S. Cultural Exchange program.

1964   Is awarded United States Medal of Freedom by
       President Johnson.

1966   *America and Americans* is published. The John Stein-
       beck Society is organized.

1968   Dies in New York City, December 20.

1969   *Journal of a Novel: The "East of Eden" Letters* is
       published.

1974   Steinbeck's boyhood home in Salinas is opened as a
       museum.

1975   *Steinbeck: A Life in Letters*, edited by Elaine Stein-
       beck and Robert Wallsten, is published.

1976   *The Acts of King Arthur and His Noble Knights* is
       published.

# 1

## The Man and His Work

Before the Nobel Prize in literature was awarded to John Steinbeck in 1962, only five Americans had been previously thus honored, the most recent being Ernest Hemingway in 1954 and William Faulkner in 1949. Steinbeck had been considered on those occasions and also in 1945 when the Chilean poet Gabriela Mistral was selected.[1] As the honor is by far the greatest any writer can receive, Steinbeck was elated. The feeling of elation was tempered slightly, however, by the observation expressed by Steinbeck in 1956, that recipients of the Nobel Prize seldom write anything of value afterwards. He cited Hemingway and Faulkner as examples, minimizing the point that by the time of their selection most writers had already written their best work.[2] Sixty himself on that occasion, Steinbeck wrote to a friend that he would not have accepted the award had he not believed that he would continue to write well, that he "could beat the rap." [3] Like his contemporaries, and others as well, however, he did not.

There was no expectation or need that the writer do so, for Steinbeck had long since made his mark in modern American literature. His fiction of the 1930s had gained national recognition, and such works as *Of Mice and Men* (1937) and *The Grapes of Wrath* (1939) had been highly acclaimed in other lands as well. These works and *Tortilla Flat* (1935), *In Dubious Battle* (1936), and *The*

*Long Valley* (1938), a collection of stories that includes
"Flight" and *The Red Pony*, reveal hallmarks of Steinbeck's fiction: sensitive and versatile craftsmanship,
keen awareness of economic and social problems, and enduring faith in mankind and compassion for the underdog.
Later works show a decline in quality with only *Cannery
Row* (1945) measuring up to prewar standards. Such
other works as *The Wayward Bus* (1947) and *East of
Eden* (1952), while at times impressive, lack the com-
mand of materials and insights into American ideas and
people of the earlier fiction. Steinbeck's last novel, *The
Winter of Our Discontent* (1961), is timely and perceptive, but it lacks the familiar California locale and reveals various flaws.

Since Steinbeck's death in 1968, the later works
have gained some critical support, while the major works,
including the nonfiction *Sea of Cortez* (1941), have lost
none of their brilliance. These works of the 1930s and
1940s represent the high points of a career that spans a
third of the twentieth century—1929 to 1966—and of a
life that is itself as engrossing and many-sided as the
fiction.

John Steinbeck grew up in California, where grandparents on both sides of the family had settled in the
mid-1800s. While traveling in Germany in the 1850s, his
paternal grandmother, Almira Ann Dickson, a New Eng-
lander, met and fell in love with a young cabinetmaker
named John Adolph Grossteinbeck. They were married
in the Holy Land. Shortly before the Civil War, they
came to America, lived in New Jersey, and then in Florida,
where Steinbeck's father, John Ernst, was born. After
serving briefly with the Confederate army, the grandfather moved with his family back to New England, and
then, perhaps originating the pattern for journeys in *To a
God Unknown* (1933) and *East of Eden* (1952), he left
for California, settling in 1874 near Hollister, where he

was soon joined by his family. The grandfather operated a flour mill and along with other family members gained a reputation for honesty and industry. In 1890 John Ernst Steinbeck, tall and strong as his son would be, moved to King City, became a bookkeeper and in 1892 married Olive Hamilton, a young schoolteacher.

Olive Hamilton's Irish parents had left Ulster in 1851 and appeared in central California soon thereafter. While the early whereabouts of the family remains obscure it is known that Olive was born in San Jose in 1866. Subsequently, the Hamiltons, prefiguring family activities in *East of Eden,* homesteaded a sprawling 1750-acre ranch east of King City. If the fictional account is reliable, the family had a difficult time growing crops and raising cattle on this land, which had little water and well holes that often dried up in the summer heat. But the vigorous, imaginative father overcame the challenges and short-comings of the land, and Olive's mother, strict and practical, instilled in members of the growing, close-knit family respect for God, Bible, and facts.

At seventeen, Olive, the fourth child, began teaching in one-room schools in the rugged coastal areas of Big Sur, below San Francisco, and reachable only on horse-back.[4] After her marriage and the second child, the family settled permanently in Salinas in 1894, where John Ernst found work at the Sperry Flour mill.

At the turn of the century Salinas was a typical American small town, differing from Faulkner's hometown in Mississippi and Hemingway's in Illinois only in location and a few distinctive features. Located about a hundred miles south of San Francisco, near Monterey Bay, Salinas in 1900 boasted a thriving population of three thousand. The town had its Main and Market Streets, a business district of four square blocks, a few restaurants and hotels, the Dashaway Stables for horses on South Main, and the Sperry Flour mill on Castroville Street.

In those years the town streets often echoed to the

noises of horse-drawn carriages and the first gas-buggies.
Winding throughout the town were narrow sloughs that
could be easily jumped or crossed on small footbridges.
In the spring and summer months frogs in the sloughs
added their croaks to the atmosphere. North of the business district and across the Southern Pacific railroad
tracks were a few distinctive features the solid citizens
of Salinas condemned: "China Town" on Soledad Street
and the town's "row," or brothels, on California Street.
As intimated in *East of Eden*, Steinbeck as a boy loitered
around the sidewalks there, peering from vacant lots to
watch the plain exteriors of the little houses and buildings. To boys his age the area was strictly off limits.
He was expected to spend all his time in his own neighborhood or in other respectable areas nearby and also to attend the white frame Episcopal church every Sunday
and the nearby schools for the lower grades.[5]

The house in which John Steinbeck was born on
27 February 1902 was a large Victorian structure with
the familiar gables and embellishments of the period. As
a fourth child, a daughter, was born a few years after
John, the family needed a spacious house. This one was
to serve the Steinbecks for some thirty years. The family
itself proved to be unusual, at least for writers of that
generation, because disruptive tensions were seemingly
few and family life appeared to be secure and happy. The
father was a quiet, kindly man involved in family affairs
and interested in his children. He was the first to recognize his son's unusual talents and to express confidence in
his promise as a writer. The mother, energetic and active
in club work, hoped that her boy would grow up to be
a banker. When she realized that John's abilities and
dreams lay elsewhere, she firmly believed that someday
he would become a successful writer like Booth Tarking-
ton, a novelist popular at that time.

Both parents regarded cultural influences as important and enjoyable aspects of life. Several times a year

the family traveled by train to San Francisco to see plays and attend concerts. As the parents were well educated and loved books, it was the custom after dinner for everyone to gather in the sitting room and listen to the father and mother take turns reading the popular Alice books, adventure stories by Robert Louis Stevenson, or tales from Greek and Roman mythology. On his ninth birthday John was delighted to receive from his father a copy of *Morte d'Arthur*.[6] It was his first book, and next to the Bible it proved to be the most influential. In later years writing what most readers regarded then and later as comic novels or social-protest fiction, Steinbeck often drew upon the Arthurian tales for ideas or materials for portraying character or shaping action, as in *Tortilla Flat* (1935) and *In Dubious Battle* (1936).

Family life in the house at 130 Central Avenue was by no means idyllic, however. The father's work as manager and owner of Sperry's mill and, later, as treasurer of Monterey County, sometimes left him impatient and out of sorts in the evening. While an understanding and realistic mother, Mrs. Steinbeck was not reluctant to make her views clear to everyone in the family. Occasional disagreements or misunderstandings were bound to occur. John and his three sisters were expected to be reasonably obedient and respectful. At the same time, they were not expected to keep out of sight or hide their talents.

The growing boy was not likely to do either. Steinbeck's boyhood was only occasionally bookish and rarely sheltered. Among the boys in that part of town, he was usually the leader—the one to start a secret society, battle imaginary foes, or lead a gang into a showdown with a rival group. A slough nearby was often a site for mud battles or fights. On more than one occasion John's vigorous leadership got him in trouble with a housewife in the neighborhood. Sometimes chores kept him occupied. The father was a good provider, but the family was not well off and John had to earn his own money. For a year or

two he carried papers for the *Morning Journal,* a job he
performed with only average proficiency, and during
high school he worked on nearby ranches during the
summers. The only welcome chore in these years began
on his twelfth birthday when his father surprised him
with a pony. The pony, named Jill, the model for Gabilan
in *The Red Pony,* was kept in the Sperry stables on
Castroville Street. Every day the boy cleaned the stall
and fed, curried, and brushed the pony that he rode in
street parades and in the large enclosure near the stable.
Ownership of the pony added to John's popularity among
his buddies.[7]

Steinbeck's lifelong interest in the mysteries and
beauty of nature began with boyhood experiences with
animals, birds, trees, and flowers which were abundant in
and outside Salinas. Family picnics and summer vacations
several miles west and north at nearby Monterey and
Pacific Grove introduced him to the shore and marine
life of Monterey Bay. Early explorations there led to
studies in college and afterwards to first-hand research of
marine life, particularly along the California coast. No
less inviting were fields and land east of Salinas. Early in
the spring John and a friend would walk out Alisal Road
and explore along the Salinas River for birds and snakes.
There were good swimming holes along the banks, small
lakes in the countryside, fields of barley and beets east of
town, and Alisal Park at the base of the Gabilan Mountains, with its old relics left by General Fremont's men
in fights with Spanish forces in the 1840s.[8]

The general locale for Steinbeck's California fiction
includes the Monterey-Salinas area, Watsonville further
north, the San Joaquin valley east of the Gabilan Mountains and in particular the Long Valley, which runs south
of Salinas for about a hundred and twenty miles and lies
between the Gabilan Mountains to the east and the
higher, craggier Santa Lucia Mountains bordering the

Pacific Ocean. Four novels and several stories are located in this area.

Steinbeck first became acquainted with the valley when he rode with others in the family car south along the Salinas River to King City, sixty miles away. The river, which begins below San Luis Obispo, actually runs north and through the middle of the valley and empties into Monterey Bay just north of Salinas. Described in several works, including *Of Mice and Men* and *East of Eden*, the Salinas River often overflows during the winter months, spreading across the valley, and runs low, frequently drying up and disappearing underground in dry months. In good years the broad, beautiful valley lands are rich with great crops of barley and lettuce, as they were in Steinbeck's youth, when from the family car he could admire broad fields on both sides of the road. In later years he worked as a ranch hand in the valley and in the 1930s wrote accounts of labor unrest there. During high school years and earlier, he hiked around the Gabilan Mountains, which were then full of deer, coyotes, rabbits, fox, squirrels, and included an occasional mountain cat and perhaps a rare bear, not to mention hawks and many other kinds of birds. The Gabilans and several small valleys would be described first in *The Pastures of Heaven* (1932) and *To a God Unknown* (1933).

High school for Steinbeck began in 1915 as he and twenty-seven others enrolled as freshmen in a two-story red-brick building. The total enrollment was two hundred. In those years high school began in the eighth grade, and in five years Steinbeck compiled a good if hardly distinguished record with B's and B pluses in most courses. By the tenth and eleventh grades he had become a tall, husky boy with fairly large features, curly brown hair, a shyness that could not hide an explosive laugh, a strong sense of humor, and a sometimes blunt honesty. As someone recalled in later years, if John did not like a class-

mate or his opinions, he told him so directly. But he was
not arrogant, and most classmates liked him. On the basis
of personal qualities, academic record, and better-than-
average performances in track and basketball, Steinbeck
was elected president of the senior class.

He was also chosen associate editor of the school newspaper, *El Gabilan*. While interesting and well written,
his articles for the newspaper gave little evidence of the
brilliance of later work. Unknown to all but a few close
friends, however, the young Steinbeck harbored literary
aspirations. Late at night, after friends had gone home
or when studying for the evening was finished and the
family was asleep, Steinbeck would write for hours in
his upstairs room. His efforts were devoted mostly to short
stories, which were mailed to magazines but with no return address, as if for the time he was afraid to receive
rejection slips. His confidence in his writing ability was
usually strong and sometimes exuberant, as it was one
day when he casually remarked to a classmate, "You
know, I write the purest English of anyone in the
world." [9] Boyish enthusiasms were sometimes not to be
contained.

English and literature courses were natural favorites
for the aspiring writer. He welcomed the opportunity to
write themes and stories, particularly on subjects of his
own choosing; and his work usually drew the attention of
the teachers. Assignments in literature were also welcome. The reading at home of novels by Flaubert, George
Eliot, Thomas Hardy, and Charles Dickens, and of the
Bible and mythology, was supplemented by equally dedicated reading at school of Shakespeare's plays, parts of
*Paradise Lost*, Chaucer's *Canterbury Tales*, English romantic poetry, and other classics—making Steinbeck at
that age more widely read than Faulkner, Hemingway,
and Fitzgerald had been in comparable years. Other fa-
vorite courses included Latin and biology, the latter
taught by an excellent teacher.

In October 1919, John Steinbeck began his somewhat checkered career at Stanford University, some eighty miles north of Salinas. If the tall gangly seventeen-year-old expected a continuation of high school successes and honors, he was not to find them. He may not in fact have sought them. Many aspects of university life were not to his liking. University regulations seemed restrictive or unnecessary. Social functions in the dormitory and elsewhere on the campus tended to be formal. The dances were always chaperoned, and John was not impressed with the beauty or friendliness of the co-eds. Hazing attempts in the dorm drew his irritation or anger. Yet he was no rebel. He was well liked by students who knew him, and two or three became lifelong friends. Planning to major in journalism, John tried to avoid some required courses but discovered like others that he could not. His athletic endeavors at Stanford went unrecognized: he did not make the freshman football team and he received only a severe knee injury for his tryout with the polo team. He finished the spring semester with average grades.

Efforts the second year proved even less rewarding. Much of the fall he spent in the university libraries reading English and Continental novels, and works by major American writers of the 1910s and 1920s, including Theodore Dreiser, Sherwood Anderson, Sinclair Lewis, and James Branch Cabell. However much John's imagination and sense of style may have benefited from the reading, class attendance and grades went down. Daily walks and bull sessions also interfered with academics. Cautions from friends and a fall notice of poor grades went unheeded. Late that fall, warned by a notice from the dean's office, Steinbeck withdrew from the university.

For two active years he remained away from Stanford. Believing at first that he had let his parents down, he avoided the Salinas area altogether, tried unsuccessfully to ship out on a San Francisco freighter, clerked in Oakland, and worked for some months in the beet and barley fields of the Willoughby ranch south of Salinas. The field work would prove invaluable fifteen years later when he began writing *Of Mice and Men* (1937). After returning to Salinas in the spring of 1922, Steinbeck lived at home, worked as a bench-chemist at the Spreckels beet factory east of town, and spent much of his free time writing. He had already decided to return to Stanford in January.

The second attempt at higher education proved successful. Determined and purposeful, Steinbeck changed his major to English, obtained permission to take the courses he wanted if these were acceptable to the department, and proceeded in the remaining three years at Stanford to get A's and B's in most courses, including composition, creative writing, English literature, French, biology, zoology, marine science, and in Greek history as well as Greek literature and philosophy. University regulations and social functions, however, left him as bored or as rebellious as ever. He preferred informal get-togethers, bull-sessions, occasional walks into town, and a girlfriend willing to share his views and sometimes his bed.

The main interest was writing. Whenever time was available, he wrote fiction and some poetry. As friends later recalled, the short stories, while not polished efforts, were entertaining and often highly imaginative. Two stories appeared in *The Stanford Spectator*: "Fingers of Cloud: A Satire on College Protervity" tells of a marriage of a subnormal girl and a migrant worker who keeps horses' heads in a rain barrel; and "Adventures in Arcademy: A Journey into the Ridiculous" is a satire of college life. Three poems also appeared in *Stanford Lit*.[10] The two stories suggest something of the mixture of realism, fantasy, and allegory characteristic of the mature Steinbeck fiction.

In June 1925, after five years of interrupted but often beneficial study, Steinbeck left the Stanford campus. He was twenty-three years old, and, unlike most classmates, had neither a degree nor prospects for a job.

His main possessions were a strong, versatile talent, many ideas for fiction, and an incomplete manuscript of what would become his first published novel, *Cup of Gold* (1929).[11]

The young writer's immediate plans that June were to finish the manuscript, which was based in part on an unpublished Stanford story entitled "A Lady in Infra-Red." For six months Steinbeck revised the manuscript at home, in the family cottage at Pacific Grove, and in Bay City near San Francisco, but for the time at least it proved unmanageable. Admitting a temporary defeat, Steinbeck went to New York City by freighter, spending most of his money en route trying unsuccessfully to charm a young woman passenger. In New York his fortunes were no more successful. He worked for six weeks as a laborer in the construction of the original Madison Square Garden, lost a job reporting for the *New York American* because his writing was too subjective, and, meantime, whenever possible, wrote fiction. Encouraged by an editor, he completed enough stories for a book, but when the editor moved to another firm the stories were returned unpublished.

Discouraged but still hopeful, Steinbeck returned to California as a deckhand on a freighter. He found more leisurely work as a caretaker at Lake Tahoe and as a fish sorter near Tahoe City. While working over the long manuscript, Steinbeck received word of his first professional publication. "The Gifts of Iban," a fantasy in the manner of the Stanford stories, appeared in March 1927, under the pseudonym of John Stern, presumably because Steinbeck did not want to be associated in any way with a magazine entitled *The Smoker's Companion*.[12]

Throughout the ups and downs of Steinbeck's long career, friends provided invaluable support and companionship. The writer was rarely without friends. Several in the 1920s were notable. Toby Street, a Stanford classmate, offered John employment after the return from

New York and gave him his own unpublished play to use
in the writing of the third novel, *To a God Unknown*.
Carleton "Dook" Sheffield, another classmate, was a helpful friend in those years. There were also women friends.
In his middle and late twenties Steinbeck, no longer gangly or awkward, was a big, roughly handsome man who
liked and needed the company of women.

The most important woman by far and a major influence in his life was Carol Henning, whom he met in
1928 and married in 1930. Carol was similarly energetic
and unpretentious. For many years, in towns in southern
California and in Pacific Grove, she worked as a typist,
secretary, and copyreader so that the author husband
could continue to write steadily. In late 1928 came the
good news that the long, much-revised manuscript had
been accepted. *Cup of Gold* was published in 1929. The
small advance for the work was welcome though it could
do little to boost their finances, particularly during the
early years of the Depression.

With ten million people out of work in 1931 and soup
kitchen lines and closed stores familiar sights in towns
and cities across the country, John Steinbeck's situation
in the early 1930s was not bad. Carol usually brought
in a small weekly check, and Steinbeck's father helped
them out with a rent-free cottage and $25 per month.
Living in Pacific Grove in the early 1930s, the young
couple could catch fish from the bay to supplement their
diet, and occasionally they could obtain vegetables and
fruit that farmers in nearby valleys could not sell.
Many friends were no better off. On an evening they
would gather at one house or another and, over wine that
sold for twenty to thirty cents a gallon, talk about
F.D.R.'s policies, the NRA, signs of labor unrest in California and elsewhere, the growing number of unem-
ployed, and about literature, art, and writing. A few
friends were members of the intellectual bohemia of the
Monterey Peninsula. These included Evelyn Ott, a psy-

chiatrist, and Joseph Campbell, an authority on mythology, who introduced Steinbeck to Jungian ideas, including archetypes that figure in later fiction. After reading the manuscript of *To a God Unknown* (1933), Campbell advised the young writer to cut down passages of philosophic speculation seemingly unrelated to the plot. Another friend and advisor, Mrs. Gregory, a longtime native of Monterey and a local historian, provided him with information on the paisanos of the area. John was to describe these people of Spanish, Indian, and Mexican blood in several works.[13]

The most important friendship of Steinbeck's life began in 1930, when he met Edward Ricketts, a marine biologist and operator of a marine laboratory in Monterey. Ricketts, unmarried and several years older, was far more interested in studying the incredible richness of animal life in the bay area and south along the California coast than in running a profitable business in town. Educated at the University of Chicago, a competent and serious scientist, and a freewheeling spirit in his own right, Ricketts provided the intellectual and emotional companionship Steinbeck needed. The two men were kindred spirits sharing interests in art, music, and literature, and to some extent in wine and women.

They shared scientific interests as well. While not trained as a scientist, Steinbeck had taken courses in marine biology, including one given at the Hopkins Marine Station in Pacific Grove, and had studied books on the subject. The activities and habitats of mollusks, crabs, octopi, and other animals along the coast had always fascinated him, and he was interested also in current ideas of such life. These included theories of the biologist William Ritter, whose studies supported the thesis that in organismal life the whole is greater than the sum of the parts. Ricketts, who believed in the thesis, contributed greatly to the writer's own understanding and use of the group-man idea.[14]

Published during these difficult but challenging years
were *Cup of Gold* (1929), *The Pastures of Heaven*
(1932), and *To a God Unknown* (1933), works bringing
neither the financial assistance nor the critical recognition
that at thirty Steinbeck believed that he deserved and
would in fact soon receive. The best of these, *The Pastures
of Heaven*, will receive attention in a subsequent chapter.
*Cup of Gold* is a fictionalized portrayal of the legendary
buccaneer Henry Morgan, whose ships roamed the Caribbean in the 1600s. The novel, full of adventure and romance, demonstrates Steinbeck's storytelling ability and
undeniable talent and imagination, but unfortunately the
characterizations and actions are too often superficial.
The more mature *To a God Unknown* tells of New England families settling in the Salinas Valley and prospering
until driven out by human failings and by drought. Several characterizations are made in depth, and descriptions
of family and ranch life are often convincing. Yet the visionary preoccupations of Joseph Wayne, the leader, and
Steinbeck's frequent failure to unify the visionary and
transcendental with the pragmatic seriously weaken the
novel.

In 1933, drawing from experiences with paisanos in
the beet factory outside Salinas and from information provided by Mrs. Gregory, Steinbeck wrote *Tortilla Flat*
(1935), a short novel about the humorous activities of
paisanos living the free and easy life in Monterey. Rejected initially by a number of publishers, *Tortilla Flat*
nonetheless became a national best-seller and for the time
made Steinbeck financially independent.

The next novel, *In Dubious Battle* (1936), is another
illustration of Steinbeck's remarkable versatility. Confident in his own ability and inventiveness, Steinbeck rarely
repeated himself. Materials for this unflinching account
of a strike in California apple fields came from Steinbeck's
first-hand knowledge of migrant workers, communist lead-

ers, farming conditions in Salinas Valley, and also from Milton's *Paradise Lost.*

In the 1930s and later, travel proved to be a necessity in Steinbeck's life, sometimes answering a characteristic restlessness of spirit and at other times providing a needed break from the strains of writing or of gathering materials for a new work. With *Tortilla Flat* and *In Dubious Battle* doing well, he and Carol could afford to take off. Buying a second-hand car in 1936, they made a brief trip to Mexico. On their return, Steinbeck resumed work on another and different treatment of migrants. *Of Mice and Men,* based on the Willoughby ranch experiences, is a realistic parable about two migrant workers, Lennie and George, who dream of someday settling on their own farm somewhere. With that book selling briskly in the spring and John not ready to write a stage version, the Steinbecks traveled by freighter through the Panama Canal, on to Philadelphia, and then to New York, where he talked with his agents, attended a large dinner party for the German writer Thomas Mann, and then, relying again upon the simplicities of freighter travel, they went to Europe, visiting England, his relatives and the ancestral home in Ireland, and then Sweden and Russia.

After returning to the states, the Steinbecks drove to Pennsylvania, where John worked with playwright George Kaufman on the stage version of *Of Mice and Men,* which appeared on Broadway in November 1937 and won the highly esteemed Drama Critics' Circle Award. The successes were now accumulating. In 1938 appeared *The Long Valley,* a collection of short fiction, including the memorable "The Chrysanthemums," "Flight," and *The Red Pony.*

The best known of Steinbeck's trips did not occur, however—at least not as customarily reported. This is the alleged journey in 1937 with Oklahoma migrants across the country on Highway 66 to California—the begin-

ning supposedly for work on *The Grapes of Wrath*. Jackson
J. Benson has recently shown that such a trip never took
place. Steinbeck did travel that route in 1937 but only
with his wife Carol, who reported later that he took no
notes on the trip. The important trip that fall—an invaluable one for the later writing of *The Grapes of Wrath*
—occurred in California, when Steinbeck spent four weeks
with Tom Collins, a manager and supervisor of camps for
migrant workers in the state. The two men travelled
some three hundred miles from Bakersfield to Needles in
the valley, living and working with Depression migrants
in fields along the way.

Familiar with migrant working conditions since high
school and Stanford days, Steinbeck in 1936 had written
seven investigative articles for the *San Francisco News* on
migrant conditions in various areas of the state. He had
proven to be a sympathetic and insightful observer. Some
time after the trip with Collins, Steinbeck undertook an
assignment with *Life* to write of migrants, but with the
understanding that he would receive only expenses.
Deeply upset and angered by what he had seen in the
camps and fields, Steinbeck wrote "Their Blood Is Strong"
and *L'Affaire Lettuceberg*, strong attacks on those considered responsible for such conditions, before settling
down to write what would become his greatest work, *The
Grapes of Wrath* (1939).[15] The novel won thousands of
readers, a Pulitzer Prize (1940), and a membership for
the author in the prestigious National Institute of Arts and
Letters.

Another significant journey lay in the immediate future. After a short exploration of San Francisco Bay fauna
in 1939, Steinbeck and his friend Ed Ricketts decided on
a more involved venture. After months of careful planning,
they and others went on a scientific expedition in 1940
into the Gulf of California to study and collect marine in-
vertebrates of the shoreline. Later, the two men collabo-
rated on a detailed log to cover the discussions and activi-

ties of the journey, and Ricketts compiled an extensive
scientific study of the many sea and shore animals. The
expedition proved invaluable because talks with Ricketts
and other experiences helped clarify Steinbeck's views of
man, nature, and their relationship. The log and scientific
study appeared as *Sea of Cortez* in December 1941, the
month of the Japanese attack on Pearl Harbor.

Almost forty, and too old to volunteer for one of the
nation's military services, Steinbeck sought to contribute
in other ways to the war effort. In collaboration with several others, he offered ideas for use by the military but
these were rejected as impractical. One idea, suggested by
General "Hap" Arnold of the U.S. Air Force, turned out
successfully. This was a book written after Steinbeck had
visited many Air Force camps and schools to observe the
training of bombardiers. *Bombs Away* (1942) was highly
effective in recruiting men for the service. It was worth
$250,000 to a Hollywood studio; all royalties were turned
over to the Air Force.

Dissatisfied with advisory or behind-the-scene roles,
Steinbeck served for six months in 1943 as correspondent
for the *New York Herald Tribune*, covering naval and
infantry combat in the Mediterranean, and at one time going ashore with assault troops in Italy. Shunning the role
of the amateur strategist or military tactician, he chose
to write human-interest stories about GI's in wartime.
The freshness and honesty of the stories and communiqués
were praised. During 1943–44, Steinbeck was also involved with others in writing the story for the successful
Alfred Hitchcock movie *Lifeboat*, starring Tallulah Bank-
head.[16]

During the war years the writer's personal fortunes
were undergoing major changes. The marriage with
Carol was breaking up, as close friends who had witnessed
the many quarrels expected. The divorce in 1942 was fol-
lowed in 1943 by Steinbeck's marriage in New Orleans
to dancer Gwen Verdon, whom he had met in California.

Perhaps because of the war, marital changes, and demands of his occupation, Steinbeck moved restlessly
about from New York City to Mexico to California and
back to New York. Planning to settle in Monterey, Steinbeck bought an old home in the town but, after living
there for a year, decided that the people were not
friendly, sold the house, and moved permanently to New
York. His only children, two boys, were born in 1944 and
1946.

Two years after the war, Steinbeck and photographer
Robert Capa traveled in Russia. The results of their collaboration, *A Russian Journal,* appeared in 1948. During
this period Steinbeck also wrote the scripts for the medio-
cre film version of *The Red Pony* and for the excellent
*Viva Zapata!*

For reasons to be considered later, Steinbeck's fiction
during these years showed a decline from the excellence
of earlier works. *The Moon Is Down* (1942), a World War
II novel about the occupation of an unidentified country,
sold well and gained Steinbeck a decoration from the
King of Norway, but it lacked realism and depth. Steinbeck was on much firmer ground with *The Wayward
Bus* (1947), a perceptive account of a busload of tourists
with varying backgrounds, who live together for a day or
two and portray roles in a realistic morality play. A highly
crafted short work, *The Pearl,* about a fated native family
in Mexico, also appeared in 1947. The low point of the
postwar years is *Burning Bright* (1950), an awkward
allegory about a childless modern couple and the consequences of the wife's impregnation by another man.

The only superior work of that period was written in
six weeks, shortly after the writer's return from the war.
*Cannery Row* (1945), dedicated to Ed Ricketts, is a humorous and sensitive portrayal of the casual life-styles of
inhabitants of the Row in Monterey in the peaceful 1930s.

Steinbeck was deeply shaken by two events in the late
1940s. His second marriage with Gwen Verdon was floun-

dering. By 1948 they had agreed upon a divorce. A greater blow awaited him. In 1948, while in the New York apartment, he received word that Ed Ricketts had been grievously injured in a car-train wreck in Monterey. Deeply upset, Steinbeck rushed to Monterey. When Ricketts died a few days later, the writer had to be given a sedative and put in bed. He later wrote a tribute to Ricketts that served as the introduction to the 1951 publication of *The Log of the Sea of Cortez*, and in 1954, as a final tribute, he created the character of Doc in *Sweet Thursday*.[17]

Attempting to forget the broken marriage and the loss of Ricketts, Steinbeck worked hard on the *Viva Zapata!* script and on a projected big book about the Salinas Valley. For months, however, recollections and loneliness plagued him. In early 1949, after returning to the Pacific Grove cottage, he met another woman who was to prove essential to his life. Elaine Scott, a talented and understanding person, helped Steinbeck find himself again. After her divorce, they were married in 1950. Steinbeck returned to the Salinas book with energy and purpose. The book, initially planned as a fictional account of his mother's family, the Hamiltons, included also a New England family, the Trasks. During the years of writing, the Trasks became prominent. The apparent failure to relate the two families and the awkward mixture of allegory and romanticism weakened an otherwise impressive work. *East of Eden* was published in 1952.

Life in New York City proved usually to Steinbeck's liking through the years. He welcomed the anonymity of the city, its tolerance for all kinds of people and activities, the opportunities in writing, publishing, and the arts. After the marriage to Elaine in 1950, Steinbeck felt natural and comfortable in routines of city life, which, for the Steinbecks, were generally quiet and moderate. Occasionally they entertained friends—writers, stage people, journalists, publishers—in the brownstone apartment

on East 72nd Street, or more often they went out to dinner or to see a play. He enjoyed standing by the third
floor window and watching people passing in the street
below. But the writer's inherent restlessness remained
dormant for only a short while. Not long after *East of
Eden* appeared in 1952, the couple traveled to Europe,
staying for some time in Italy, where Steinbeck reported
for *Collier's* his arguments with Italian communist leaders; participated in the opening of the Venice Biennial
Art Exhibition, devoted to American painting that year;
revisited the birthplace of his mother's parents in Ireland
in 1953; and spent much of 1954 in Paris, where, among
other things, he contributed a weekly column to *Figaro*.
The next year, desiring a yearly change from the intensity of New York, the Steinbecks bought a summer
home in Sag Harbor, Long Island, close to the sights and
sounds of the ocean. He later called it Cannery Row East.
There in relative simplicity they spent many happy
months.[18]

Before the 1950s, the writer's political views were
generally submerged in the fiction or expressed indirectly.
Early in the 1950s, Steinbeck turned to more direct expression, objecting strongly, for example, to the tactics of
Wisconsin Senator Joseph McCarthy, and in Paris writing
a much reprinted indictment of McCarthy's ideas and actions. Impressed by speeches of Adlai Stevenson, the lib-
eral Democratic standard-bearer of the 1950s, Steinbeck
helped write speeches for the 1952 and 1956 presidential
campaigns, and in the fight for the Democratic nomination in 1956 he chaired an advisory committee to Governor
Stevenson. For some years a friend also of Senator Lyn-
don Johnson of Texas, Steinbeck vigorously campaigned
for him in the 1964 campaign and later served as an advisor to President Johnson.

The Viet Nam conflict involved Steinbeck in several
ways. His older boy Thom served in the conflict, and initially Steinbeck supported the American effort there and

President Johnson's Viet Nam policies. But after further consideration following a visit to Viet Nam at age sixty-four, he changed his views and advised the president to pull out American troops. For service during those years John Steinbeck received in 1964 the United States Medal of Freedom. There were also literary awards: the Nobel Prize in 1962; the appointment, in 1963, along with Katherine Anne Porter, Saul Bellow, and Richard Eberhart, as honorary consultant in American literature to the Library of Congress; the appointment in 1964 as trustee of the John F. Kennedy Memorial Library; and in 1966, election to the National Arts Council.

The decline in quality of Steinbeck's fiction, evident in the 1940s, continued with the appearance in 1954 of *Sweet Thursday*, a third and last look at Cannery Row in Monterey. But that world, alas, has grown respectable: Doc, for example, gains a position at the California Institute of Technology, and the fantasy fails. Under the title *Pipe Dream*, it was produced as a musical by Rodgers and Hammerstein in 1955. Another comedy, *The Short Reign of Pippin IV* (1957), is an allegorical satire of the French political scene of the 1950s. Concerned as always with the moral climate in America, Steinbeck wrote the more substantial but flawed *The Winter of Our Discontent* (1961), set in a Long Island town and centered on the contrast between impressive things of the past and the much diminished versions of the present.

An important concern in the later years was the study and translation of Malory's *Morte d'Arthur*. In the late 1950s, Steinbeck spent many months in England, translating parts of the work, published posthumously as *The Acts of King Arthur and His Noble Knights* (1976).

During his last decade Steinbeck remained active in other ways as well. The longtime interest in marine science had not diminished. In 1961 he was selected as the historian for Project Mohole off the coast of Mexico. This expedition aboard *Cuss 1* was designed to study a core of

the earth's surface, and Steinbeck was delighted to be
involved. His account of it for *Life* appeared 14 April
1961. There were also plans for a scientific expedition to
the great barrier reef off the coast of Australia and another expedition with Bascom, the Mohole project leader,
to South America, but other obligations canceled these
plans.[19] Earlier, in 1960, disappointed over Adlai Stevenson's loss of the Democratic nomination, and feeling,
perhaps rightly, that as a writer and person he had lost
touch with the country, Steinbeck went on a nationwide
journey in a small trailer truck with his French poodle.
*Travels with Charley in Search of America* (1962), an absorbing account of the writer's experiences, expresses
frank and generally affirmative views of places and people. Steinbeck's love of the country and its people appear
also in the lavishly illustrated *America and Americans*
(1966), which describes American myths and achievements as the writer saw them.

Despite his strong constitution, Steinbeck was showing definite signs of aging and weakening in these years.
He suffered a stroke in 1961, from which he recovered
with no serious ill effects. In 1963 he had an operation for
a detached retina, and in 1965 he suffered another
minor stroke. A painful back condition necessitated a
spinal fusion in late 1967. After each recovery Steinbeck
continued to write letters, read, see friends, travel a little, and plan, if skeptically, for the future. On 20 December 1968, however, after a series of strokes, John
Steinbeck died peacefully in his New York apartment.
His ashes were buried in the family cemetery in Salinas.

# 2

# The Steinbeck Territory

Like William Faulkner and Willa Cather, John Steinbeck wrote his best fiction about the region in which he grew up and the people he knew from boyhood. Faulkner based the mythical Yoknapatawpha County of his many works on lands and people around Oxford, Mississippi, and on the town itself. Cather, in her most enduring novels and stories, often drew materials from Red Cloud, Nebraska, and the surrounding farmlands.

Far more extensive than Faulkner's county or Cather's homeland, the Steinbeck territory covers thousands of square miles in central California, particularly in the Long Valley, which extends south of Salinas, Steinbeck's hometown, for over one hundred miles and lies between the Gabilan Mountains on the east and the Santa Lucia Mountains along the Pacific coast. The territory includes also several small valleys along the coast as well as towns and villages scattered over a wide area, including Monterey and Pacific Grove, northwest of Salinas and overlooking the bay; Watsonville near the Santa Cruz Mountains; Salinas itself; and, south in the Valley, Soledad, King City, and Jolon. East of the Valley and the Gabilan Mountains, but still within the territory, lies the San Joaquin Valley—a principal site of Steinbeck's greatest work, *The Grapes of Wrath* (1939). Along the California coast lie tidal basins that provide materials for works dramatically relating man and his environment.

Most of Steinbeck's major works occur within this territory. The Long Valley is the general locale for "The Chrysanthemums" (1937), *Of Mice and Men* (1937), *The Red Pony* (1938), and *East of Eden* (1952). Monterey is the site for *Tortilla Flat* (1935), *Cannery Row* (1945), and *Sweet Thursday* (1954), and Watsonville and a nearby valley serve in *In Dubious Battle* (1936). Referred to in many stories and novels, Salinas is the setting for a part of *East of Eden*. Soledad in the Valley may be the town referred to in *Of Mice and Men*; and King City, where Steinbeck's parents were married in 1892, is another source of materials for *East of Eden*. The nonfiction *Sea of Cortez* (1941) deals with the Gulf of California and Mexico, and several stories and parts of *Cannery Row* include actions set in the tidal basins near Monterey.[1]

Appearing in a career of over thirty years are works located in other areas as well, including the Caribbean, the eastern United States, France, a hypothetical Norway, and Russia. A few of these—*Sea of Cortez* (1941) and *The Pearl* (1947)—are excellent, and *The Winter of Our Discontent* (1961) has its strengths. The strongest fiction, however, reflects the great range and diversity of Steinbeck's main territory through the varieties of nationalities, characters, and occupations. In the territory appear Mexicans, Spanish, and Chinese, as well as German, Irish, and English; not only ranchers and farmers but also migrant workers, community leaders, assorted whores and bums, as well as fishermen, bartenders, schoolteachers, and radicals. The characters include the wealthy, poor, and economically in-between; the able, bigoted, mature, puritanic, psychotic, and happy. The vast territory is a factor also in shaping dominant themes in the fiction, including man's relationships with the land, the attractions of the simple life, the conflicts of the haves and have-nots, the failures or dangers of middle-class existence.

The breadth and richness of the territory are not

touched on in Steinbeck's first novel, *Cup of Gold* (1929), with its accounts of pirates and adventures in the Caribbean, but in works immediately following appear the first explorations. These include *The Pastures of Heaven* (1932), *To a God Unknown* (1933), *Tortilla Flat* (1935), and a collection of stories, *The Long Valley* (1938). *Tortilla Flat*, Steinbeck's first major work and first study of a town, will be considered later in this chapter. Space does not allow for a detailed consideration of *To a God Unknown*, set in Nacimiento River Valley far south of Monterey and centered on the Wayne brothers, who migrate from New England in the early 1900s and settle on isolated Valley land. While frontier times lie in the past, the Waynes and their families show pioneering courage and resourcefulness in subduing the land and making it productive. In time, however, personal and family differences and a relentless drought combine to drive them from the land.

Written between 1932 and 1938, stories of *The Long Valley* provide an excellent introduction to the varieties of the territory: five are set in the Long Valley, or an adjacent area; five in towns and one in the coastal mountains; only "Saint Katy the Virgin" occurs outside the territory. While in most of the stories the relationship of man and land is secondary or is treated superficially, a few stories delve into the relationship, anticipating the searching examinations of man and land in *In Dubious Battle*, *Of Mice and Men*, and particularly *The Grapes of Wrath*. The stories serve also to illustrate Steinbeck's early commitment to craftsmanship: a sensitive and supple prose style; various unifying patterns, and a range in treatment from the realistic to the allegorical and symbolic.

The first three stories of the collection are among Steinbeck's best known and most expertly written short works. They are notable also for what they illustrate of the locales and characters in the territory. The first story, "The Chrysanthemums," begins with a detailed description of the rich Salinas Valley:

The high grey-flannel fog of winter closed off the Salinas Valley from the sky and from all the rest of the world. On every side it sat like a lid on the mountains and made of the great valley a closed pot. On the broad, level land floor the gang plows bit deep and left the black earth shining like metal where the shares had cut. On the foothill ranches across the Salinas River, the yellow stubble fields seemed to be bathed in pale cold sunshine, but there was no sunshine in the valley now in December.

On one foothill ranch live the Allens, a middle-aged, childless couple, seemingly successful with their ranch and their marriage. As the story opens, Elisa Allen works in the flower garden as her husband Henry completes a sale of thirty steers to buyers for a meat company. To celebrate the sale, the couple decide to spend the evening in Salinas. As Elisa expertly prepares new chrysanthemum sprouts from old roots, an itinerant repairman of kitchenware arrives unexpectedly. Although no work is available, Elisa finds pans for repair after the man plays on her pride. She responds strongly also to accounts of his way of life. The tinker soon leaves with a half dollar for his work and a flower pot of sprouts for someone down the road. Later, Elisa becomes upset after discovering the discarded sprouts and dirt lying on the road.

The outward contentment and security of the ranch hide the loneliness and frustration of a woman who may love her husband but feels little warmth in the relationship. The simple story outlines are enriched by irony and imagery which contrast the rich land and the sterile marriage, the fertile plants and Elisa's inner emptiness. The skillful dialogue underlines the contrasts: the husband's inept remarks about prize fights and breaking steers and

the tinker's imaginative remarks about flowers. Although
quick to praise his wife's gardening skill, Henry can say
nothing warm and affectionate about her attractiveness.
The tinker, while sensing her inner frustration and need,
responds by misleading remarks and actions. The garden
imagery suggests both Elisa's partial fulfillment and her
deep sexual frustration. The plants and flowers cannot
compensate for the lack of understanding and affection
from her husband. She reaches out toward the stranger,
but does not reach, actually or figuratively, toward her
husband. Riding in the car that evening, Elisa feels separated from both Henry and the tinker. The trip itself, unlike the tinker's, is to no new horizon but only to Salinas
and back. Clearly all is not well in Steinbeck's Eden.

The locale in "The White Quail," the second story,
shifts to "the very edge of" a town where Mary Teller and
her husband Harry live. As in "The Chrysanthemums,"
the couple is childless and the wife is preoccupied with a
garden. Before her marriage, Mary had dreamed of a
beautiful house and garden and a husband to match. The
dream has materialized, for she has an adoring husband,
a lovely home, and a beautiful and perfectly arranged
garden, an embodiment she believes of her own beauty
and goodness. When a white quail begins appearing
nightly in the garden, Mary's happiness is complete, for,
as she explains to Harry, "She's like me." But soon a
threatening cat begins appearing in the garden. Mary insists that Harry shoot the cat. For reasons he cannot understand, the usually obliging husband shoots instead the
white quail.

Mary Teller's identification with garden and quail indicates far deeper problems than Elisa's. Mary's self love,
which is reflected in her obsessions with the garden and
the quail, is so intense that it seems to wall out Harry
and their married life. At night Mary frequently locks the
door between the bedrooms. Her fear or dislike of sex and

of the world beyond the house and beautiful garden is hidden by beautiful manners and by an immaculate way of
life.

While sensitively written and carefully crafted,
"The White Quail" lacks the vitality and depth of "The
Chrysanthemums," perhaps because of the allegorical
emphasis: the garden and white quail are fixed symbols
of Mary's ideal qualities; the cat and the "dark thickets of
the hill" represent threats and dangers in herself or
others. On the surface Mary Teller is a skillfully drawn
character, a familiar Steinbeck figure who loses contact
with the real world. But the actual nature of Mary's fear
and repression is left vague. So too is the unconscious rage
of the deeply frustrated husband who at the end can only
blame himself.

The locale of the excellent story "Flight" is not a
fertile valley or a peaceful town, but an area "about fifteen miles below Monterey, on the wild coast" and inland
over rugged mountain terrain. The small Torres farm is
situated on the mountain slopes above a cliff that drops to
the sea. Mama Torres and her three children eke out a sub-
sistence-level life on the sterile land, the father having
died years before from a rattlesnake bite. Mama Torres
hopes that her oldest child, Pepé, a tall, lazy youth of
nineteen, skillful with his knife, will someday become the
man in the family. On a Sunday morning she sends him
on an errand to Monterey, where he kills a man with his
knife. Upon returning, Pepé is given his father's coat and
rifle and rides off on his father's horse into the mountains. With pursuers somewhere behind him and dark
watchers on the cliffs, Pepé flees inland. He must contend
also with nature. At last, badly wounded and alone, Pepé
can do no more than stand up bravely and be shot by
an unseen pursuer.

Richer and more complex than "The Chrysanthemums" or "The White Quail," "Flight" is a story of several levels. The barren slopes farmed by the Torres fam-

ily, Pepé's flight from his pursuers, the rugged, sometimes dangerous mountain terrain, the wild animals, and Pepé's physical deterioration are all described in firm, realistic prose. Scene, action, and character are solidly presented. The symbolic level is no less convincing and illustrates the story's ironies. Pepé's flight or escape leads to his manhood, but it leads also to his death. The primitive nature into which he flees is destructive as well as protective. The youth copes as well as he can with both human pursuers and nature's dangers. The mountain lion suggests both the animality toward which Pepé is slipping and a source of death he does not escape. The story is also enriched by allegorical elements: the father's possessions which Pepé gradually loses as he goes further into danger and approaches his own manhood; the dark watchers who stand for death as well as society's laws. The journey itself is both fact and symbol, an impressive reworking of such traditional themes as the flight from society into the wild, the passage from innocence to experience, the painful growth to maturity. All such aspects of the story are unified by the dramatic focus in each scene and on Pepé's increasingly difficult predicament.

Of the less skillful stories in *The Long Valley*, several dramatize small-town situations in the territory and illustrate forms of adaptability and violence. They are weakened by Steinbeck's tendency to create allegorical figures designed principally to express an idea, attitude, or emotion. His interest in noticeably abstract portrayals too often results in a character whose personality or motivations appear unconvincing.[3] This is evident in "The Snake" as a woman visits Dr. Phillips in his Monterey laboratory, buys a rattlesnake, and then languidly observes its actions in devouring a rat. The doctor is believable, but the woman, representing evil or snakelike primitive qualities, is not. "The Raid," another tightly written story set in a town, anticipates *In Dubious Battle* by its portrayal of violence and economic conflict, but the idealism

of the two radicals is more explainable in allegorical
than in psychological terms. "The Vigilante," a story of a
small-town man and his reactions to a lynching, probes
character more effectively and interestingly relates sex
and violence. A town and the surrounding community are
treated in some detail in "Johnny Bear." The title figure is
a gifted idiot whose verbalized recollections to patrons of
the town bar reveal the failings of the aristocratic Haw-
kins sisters, hitherto regarded by most everyone in Loma
as puritanical and untouchable.

The remaining stories in *The Long Valley* include
"Saint Katy the Virgin," a humorous satire involving a
sow and the Catholic Church, seemingly out of place in
the collection; "Breakfast," a sketch reappearing in *The
Grapes of Wrath*, and two stories, "The Harness" and
"The Murder," about unhappy childless farm couples. In
"The Harness," Peter Randall, a highly respected
farmer, straight and broad-shouldered, breaks down over
the death of his crippled, sickly wife. He reveals afterwards to a neighbor that for twenty-one years his wife
had dominated him, even requiring that he wear a belt
and harness to keep him straight and slim. Trying to escape the domination, Randall dresses as he pleases, farms
as he wants, and lives it up in San Francisco—only to
discover that he cannot escape. In a contrasting account,
Jim Moore in "The Murder" finds his wife Jelka docile
and pliant. As she appears indifferent sexually, Jim visits
Monterey weekly until one night he discovers Jelka and
her male cousin asleep in bed. Jim shoots the man and informs the sheriff. The next day, after an unusual reconcil-
iation with Jelka, Jim plans to build a new home further
south in the Valley.

The highlight of the collection is *The Red Pony*, an
excellent short novel, which more fully than any other
work except *The Grapes of Wrath*, published the following year, examines the relationship of man and the land.
Jody Tiflin, a bright, imaginative ten-year-old, is keenly

interested in most things and activities on the farm in the Valley. In the first part, "The Gift," the boy does his chores dutifully, plays on the farm, and goes to school. One morning he is surprised and overjoyed when his strict father gives him a red pony for his birthday. With the help of Billy Buck, the hired hand, Jody takes good care of the pony. But as mistakes occur, the pony dies. In "The Great Mountain," a stranger, an old Mexican, Gitano, unexpectedly visits the farm, to die, he explains, on the site of his birth. While Mrs. Tiflin and Jody want him to remain, the father allows him to stay only overnight. The next day, as Gitano disappears heading west, Jody, usually curious about the mountains, feels only a sense of loss. In "The Promise," in order to get another colt Jody pays a stud fee and works all summer. At the delivery, Billy discovers that to save the colt he must kill the mare. Although frightened by the upsetting scene, Jody does not leave. The last part, "The Leader of the People," tells of the visit of Mrs. Tiflin's father, a friendly old man whose stories about "westering" are familiar to all. Jody loves them, Billy is sympathetic, but Carl's impatience is plain to see. The grandfather confesses to Jody that he only wishes others to know how he and his followers felt then.

Unlike the luckless Pepé in "Flight," Jody grows up on good, fertile land, benefits from a secure family life, and survives his encounters with death and unpredictable nature. Steinbeck's accounts of Jody's life and survival show a similarly graceful and detailed realism. We gain a firm impression of the outward boy, his playing with Doubletree Mutt, deference to his parents, and a close relationship with Buck. The sensitive language and point of view create a sense also of the inner Jody, of his daydreams about armies marching down the country road behind him, of the large colt next to Nellie:

And then he saw himself breaking a large colt to halter. All in a few moments the colt grew to be a magnificent animal, deep of chest, with a neck as high and arched as a sea-horse's neck, with a tail that tongued and rippled like black flame. This horse was terrible to everyone but Jody. In the schoolyard the boys begged rides, and Jody smilingly agreed. But no sooner were they mounted than the black demon pitched them off.

Descriptions of farm activities, the countryside, and other people are inseparable from descriptions of a boy growing up. The descriptions, point of view, concentration on the farm scenes and activities and on Jody in particular unify the four parts of the novel.

Adults in the work are portrayed with considerable skill. The mother, variously affectionate, concerned, and exasperated, is more credible than the strict but nonetheless involved father. Billy Buck, impressively and realistically created, provides Jody with the necessary day-by-day attention. Learning from experience like Hemingway's young Nick Adams, but more soundly prepared by farm life and his elders, Jody Tiflin learns that dying is natural and living requires sacrifices. Like Nick he learns also that forces in nature can be unpredictable and dangerous. The closing scenes of *The Red Pony* dramatize Jody's maturing tolerance for others and indicate that eventually he will outgrow his teachers.

Steinbeck's first major work, *The Pastures of Heaven* (1932), centers on a limited area of the fictional territory. Located some twelve miles from Monterey, the Corral de Tierra was a familiar valley to Steinbeck in his boyhood. In the late 1920s the valley was the site of activities which became the basis of *The Pastures of Heaven*. As Steinbeck explained in 1931 to his publisher, twenty families were living peacefully in the beautiful valley "in the hills" until a new family arrived, and, without being unkindly or malicious, caused "two murders, a suicide, many quarrels and a great deal of unhappiness." [4]

Such events and materials deeply impressed the

writer who recreated them in the light of his own experiences and powerful imagination. The locale remains the Corral de Tierra. Discovered in 1776 by a Spanish Corporal who named it "Las Pasturas del Cielo," the valley had been settled in the 1860s by the Battle family and others, and much later by the Mustrovics. As the Battle family died on the farm and the Mustrovics fled from it, the farm carried a curse. Ignoring the curse, the Munroes in the 1920s buy the farm and proceed innocently to bring sorrow or failure to others in the valley. Shark Wicks is the first to suffer. His reputation as a financial wizard is shattered as a consequence of Jimmie Munroe's interest in Wicks's daughter. Next is Tularecito, a powerful idiot with remarkable drawing ability, who is committed to a state institution after he attacks Bert Munroe. Mrs. Helen Van Deventer and her emotionally disturbed daughter, Hilda, newcomers to the valley, are briefly visited by neighbor Bert, whose good intentions but thoughtless remarks lead to the daughter's death. Junius Maltby and his son enjoy their simple, imaginative farm life until Mrs. Munroe and others confront them with economic facts; they are compelled to depart. The Lopez sisters and Molly Morgan leave the valley because of remarks made by Bert Munroe, and John Whiteside's mansion is destroyed by fire after Bert insists that nearby brush be burned. In the epilogue, a busload of tourists, gazing on the beautiful valley, indulge in their own farfetched dreams of happy life there.

While *The Pastures of Heaven* is skillfully written, several aspects appear only partly satisfying. The unity itself is problematic, for the work can be regarded as a collection of stories or as a loosely organized novel. If it is the first, such factors as the locale or territory, the ironies of existence in the valley, and the Munroes are not sufficiently pervasive to unify the different episodes within one general narrative. The related aspects of locale and irony can be considered first.

Many scenes and activities in "Las Pasturas del Cielo" evoke a sense of peace and fulfillment. The first and last chapters—the prologue and epilogue, in effect—enclose the action with descriptions of abundance and fertility. In chapter 1 we read that "their land was rich and easy to work, the fruit of their gardens were the finest produced in central California." This description, referring to the 1860s, applies as well to the 1920s. Many families and individuals in the valley find freedom to express themselves. Tularecito has a natural way with animals and hopes, ironically, to find his friends in the good earth. Junius Maltby and Robbie enjoy their lazy farm life, and the prosperity and well-being of Raymond Banks are due in large measure to the land. Pat Humbert loves the farmland, and works to forget the house and its memories. Seeking to overcome his own bad luck elsewhere, Bert Munroe becomes a prosperous farmer and "a part of the valley." Even the obsessed Helen Van Deventer finds occasional solace and peace of mind in her garden. With their history and tradition, the Whitesides are most indebted to the land and valley and in turn expect the most from it. Others, like the Lopez sisters and Molly Morgan, less directly related to the land, nonetheless benefit for a time from its peacefulness and security.

The beautiful valley, however, contains hidden and overt curses: the corporal dies of the pox; the Battle and Mustrovic families eventually disappear; and the Battle farm was

always sodden with gloom and with threatening. The trees which grow up around a deserted house are dark trees, and the shadows they throw on the ground have suggestive shapes. . . . The weeds, with a holiday energy, free of fear of the hoe, grew as large as small trees.

The spectre of gloom and threat that spreads over the valley may arise also from a less palpable curse: the harmful effects of middle-class standards and expectations.

It is this particular irony—as much as any other single factor—that pervades and unifies the different actions and shapes the fates of the characters involved. Thus, we find in the beautiful valley a man like Wicks, who, in attempting to maintain a reputation as financial wizard, succeeds only in hurting himself and his family. Tularecito loses his freedom because he lacks the mentality to understand middle-class community laws governing education and property rights. Indifference to standards of personal appearance and farm maintenance leads to Maltby's departure from the valley. Even though Pat Humbert takes good care of his land, he cannot through work escape psychological burdens. John Whiteside discovers that family traditions, achievements, and ideals will not perpetuate the dynasty. A numerous and like-minded progeny is essential.

The extent to which the ubiquitous Munroes serve to unify the actions and ironies of the work is difficult to determine. It is unlikely that they serve only to pass on the curse of the Battle farm, for, as several critics have pointed out, the main curse lies in the harmful effects of middle-class respectability.[5] There is the view that the Munroes innocently hurt others through their own callous goodwill and that each succeeding example of such will is worse than the last. If so, such a rising development would fundamentally unify the novel.[6] However, this does not seem to be the case. Later actions do not appear worse than preceding ones, and some appear contrived or merely coincidental. Thus, Bert Munroe happens to fill in the holes dug by Tularecito, and Pat Humbert happens to overhear Mae Munroe's remark to her mother. Bert's jokes at the expense of Maria Lopez and Allen Hueneker and his neurotic reactions to Banks do not appear to be in character. In other incidents, the innocently harmful Munroes do serve to relate characters and illustrate basic ironies and thus to strengthen the impression of the work as a loosely unified novel.

This unity gains some support throughout from characters whose reactions to their ultimate predicaments in
the lovely valley are determined by dreams and obsessions.[7] In the beginning, Shark Wicks gets along well with
neighbors and family by appearing to be someone he is
not. His obsessions with this role impair family relations,
mislead others, and eventually lead to the departure of the
entire family. Helen Van Deventer's dreamworld appears
more complex. Since the age of fifteen she has accepted
tragedy as a way of life, and regarded herself as equal to
any burden. Yet her husband's death and Hilda's abnormality compel her to hide inside a fortress-cabin with a
memorial room for her husband and a cell-room for her
daughter. Ironically, the beautiful Helen is as abnormal as
her daughter and no less capable of violence. To keep
others from destroying the dream, she destroys part of it
herself.

Pat Humbert and Molly Morgan also live to some extent in dreams that are harmful to no one except to themselves. Like Wicks and Helen Van Deventer, they have
views of reality strongly conditioned by the past.[8] Pat,
shy and kindly, tries to escape the grim reminders of his
parents by participating in group activities in the
valley. But at home Pat shuns the closed-up parlor and
lives in the kitchen except when he is outside working.
That the frightened man eagerly seeks someone to relate
to is shown in his obsessed attempts to create a dream
house for a dream girl he does not know. When the
dream is destroyed, Pat Humbert is all but broken. Molly
Morgan, in many ways realistic and adaptable, is highly
regarded in the valley as a teacher and as a person. Her
unhappy family life and dreams of a desolate father, however, have conditioned her views of reality. The Whitesides provide the love and security Molly did not find at
home, but she cannot face the fact that her father has
always been a drifter. To maintain her illusion of him as

an adventurer and a good father, she sacrifices her happiness and position in the community.

Another group of characters in the peaceful valley includes those who because of some lack of intelligence, temperament, or imagination fall short of valley or middle-class standards. Their fates reinforce the thematic unity of the action. Left on the ranch with Gomez, Tularecito would do all right, for he has a natural way with animals and plants. But as his remarkable abilities and natural simplicity are not balanced by adequate intelligence, Tularecito remains oblivious of the expectations of others. When faced with an unmanageable situation, the Lopez sisters do not respond with violence, as does Tularecito, but with affection or sex. Unlike Tularecito they harm no one. Like him, they are unaware of community standards: in this instance, the various prohibitions against prostitution. Thus, they, too, must leave the valley. Raymond Banks, in contrast, is admired throughout the community for exemplary farm management and hospitality. Yet the man is singularly unimaginative, He kills chickens with remarkable efficiency, plays a Santa Claus who does not laugh, and attends prison hangings to share the reactions of others. After Bert cruelly enlightens him, Banks may change his naive attitude toward violence.

Junius Maltby and John Whiteside represent contrasting extremes in the valley. Not interested in improving or even maintaining his farm, Junius is regarded by many as shiftless or incompetent. To others he appears indifferent to his son's welfare. Junius is also poor. The wealthy John Whiteside is the acknowledged community leader whose family history and position give the valley a sense of identity. The Whiteside home is a symbol of leadership and tradition. Both men are intelligent, educated, and seemingly happy or content. Maltby lives the simple peaceful life with an emphasis on imagination and individual expression. His children die, however, except

for one who grows up with similar qualities and needs.
Whiteside loves books, too, but for what they tell him of
classical times and family activities. Whiteside, wishing to
perpetuate the family dynasty, has only one child who,
sharing none of his father's interests, finds his future in
the town. Neither Maltby's seemingly ineffectual way
of life nor Whiteside's honored traditions and leadership
can survive the influence of the valley, the influences of
the Munroes. Middle-class respectability inevitably has its
victims.

*Tortilla Flat,* Steinbeck's first nationally recognized
work, appeared in 1935. The manuscript had been rejected
by publishers who regarded it as an amusing collection of
stories with no apparent purpose or unity, and with little
appeal for readers during the Depression. The publishers
were mistaken. *Tortilla Flat* quickly appeared on national best-seller lists and made Steinbeck financially independent. But critical comments that the novel lacked a
significant unity disturbed Steinbeck, for he had drawn
parallels between adventures in *Tortilla Flat* and in
Malory's *Morte d'Arthur* in order to provide such unity.[9]
Later, to answer criticism and clarify purpose and structure in the book, he added to the second edition a preface
which begins:

This is the story of Danny and of Danny's friends and of
Danny's house . . . of how these three became one thing. . . .
Danny's house was not unlike the Round Table, and Danny's
friends were not unlike the knights of it. And this is the story
of how that group came into being, of how it flourished and
grew to be an organization beautiful and wise.

The preface provides also an important description of Monterey and a definition of paisano, the nationality of most
of the novel's characters, as someone with "a mixture of
Spanish, Indian, Mexican, and assorted Caucasian bloods."
The equivalent term today is Chicano.

These various materials are presented with far more dramatic concentration than is evident in *The Pastures of Heaven*. The focus is always on Danny, his friends, and their activities. *Tortilla Flat* begins with Danny's return from World War I to discover that he is the owner of two houses in Tortilla Flat, the upper part of Monterey. Not caring for the responsibility, he goes on a lark, is jailed, escapes, and meets his old friend Pilon, who agrees to share the responsibility and also to pay rent. Somehow he never does. To ease his conscience Pilon allots part of one house to Pablo and Jesus Maria, who also agree to pay rent but never do.

Parties in the houses are frequent and merry. After Pilon's house burns down during one spree, everyone moves in with Danny. Later, the friends admit into their group the Pirate, his five dogs, and his treasure of two hundred dollars in quarters. All agree that the treasure is not to be touched. When Portagee Joe steals a few quarters, he is thoroughly beaten. After several weeks of changeless life, Danny disappears, roams unfettered, is jailed, and, upon his release, is given a big party during which he performs legendary feats. Then, dashing out into the night, he falls into the gulch and is killed. Many attend the funeral, but the friends, who lack suitable clothing, cannot. Afterwards, they walk away, "no two . . . together."

As such a summary suggests, *Tortilla Flat* may be considered an episodic novel centered around contrast between the life-styles of Danny and friends and the standards of middle-class Monterey. *Tortilla Flat* shows qualities also of a modern picaresque, for Danny and friends are humorous rogues of the 1930s whose escapades and travels in and around the city provide comments on themselves and other paisanos and on people living south of the Flat.

Underlying such patterns is a partly literal, partly figurative structure, brilliantly explained by Fontenrose,

which provides the most consistent unity in *Tortilla Flat*.[10]
This is the elaboration of Malory parallels and materials
referred to in the preface and surfacing more or less
visibly in the chapters. Chapter titles, descriptions of
characters, dialogue, and the overall progression of the action often bear close if ironic resemblances to the materials. As the *Morte d'Arthur* is a monumental narrative,
only a few highlights will be mentioned here to clarify
likely resemblances or parallels. Early in the adventures
King Arthur receives from Guinevere a wedding gift of
one hundred knights and a round table. The Knights
of the Round Table are soon united in fighting enemy in-
vaders and foreign nations, and in rescuing the enslaved
or imprisoned. The greatest knight is Launcelot, the fa-
vorite of Queen Guinevere. Launcelot and other knights
quest for the Holy Grail; Launcelot's son Galahad succeeds. Because of his love for Guinevere, Launcelot leaves
Camelot, and returns only to avenge King Arthur's
death. Fontenrose's explanation of the many parallels between the Steinbeck and Malory materials reveals a depth
and an overall unity earlier unknown.

Since the novel is set in the California 1930s, however, and the locale is usually the Flat, the enriching and
unifying parallels are not to be taken literally. Descriptions of Danny's rickety houses, the stunted trees, the piles
of ashes and junk, and of other houses and yards elsewhere leave no doubt of the economic level. The times are
hard. Yet, as Steinbeck's purpose in *Tortilla Flat* is more
involved than in *The Pastures of Heaven*, the prose style
is accordingly complex, being not only realistic and factual but subtly ironic and poetic as well. Descriptions of
Danny's second house, the better of the two, are illustrative:

Danny and Pilon stood in front of the paintless picket
fence and looked with admiration at the property, a low
house streaked with old whitewash, uncurtained windows
blank and blind. But a great pink rose of Castile was on the

porch, and grandfather geraniums grew among the weeds in the front yard.

The details, at once precise and impressionistic, create a sense of a bare subsistence level—the drab fence, the plain house with bare windows—and of bright colors, beauty, even hope. Descriptions of the main room, with its stove and battered rocking chairs, its old calendar of 1906, tacked-up paper roses, and strings of dusty red peppers and garlic, are also ironic and humorous, for Danny and Pilon admire these as well. The prose style of *Tortilla Flat* is Steinbeck's most accomplished before *Of Mice and Men*. The ironic overtones are essential to the creation of a 1930s mock-heroic narrative: the satiric and comic portrayal of characters and activities far from admirable or noble.

Thus, we find that each house, with its broken-down porch and rose of Castile, is a place of dreams, tall tales, and grubby facts. The characters boast of their prowess and great feats; their actions, however, are trivial or ludicrous. Battles with dragons and rebellious lords become in *Tortilla Flat* occasional raids on Mrs. Morales' chicken house next door or stealthy forays along the alleys of Monterey for wine or food. The long search in the forest for the Holy Grail leads Pilon, the realist or Launcelot, to a buried U.S. Geodetic marker. King Arthur himself, or Danny, has curved legs, and his devoted knights are devoted to little besides sleeping, storytelling, fighting, and drinking. They are also chasers after women, or waiters for them, a jug of stolen wine being their usual enticement. The counterparts of lovely maidens of the Arthurian tales are lean, hip-swinging Sweets Ramirez, a likely Demon woman, who changes lovers frequently, or the always available Teresina, who may be Guinevere. Danny and Pilon respond also to the charms of Mrs. Torrelli, who, while her husband is away, provides them with dinner and stolen kisses.

While mock-heroic and realistic materials are effectively unified in *Tortilla Flat,* Steinbeck's sympathies for
the economically deprived figures and their simple, un-
cluttered lives make for some ambivalence in treatment.
Critics have pointed out that portrayals of mock-heroic or
satiric elements and of the simple, good, pastoral life do
not mix.[11] While this is a complex and not necessarily convincing point, it is pertinent and deserves a brief clarifica-
tion.

This can be done in terms of an important configuration in Steinbeck's fiction, the notion of the group-
man: a character in a group who takes on group qualities
and loses individualistic ones. As all group-men act together, or do so theoretically, the group becomes in effect an organism and acts in the simplified ways of one.
The first significant use or statement of this idea appears in
*Tortilla Flat,* for we read in the preface that the paisanos
are parts of a unit, that they act together on the basis of
"friendship, loyalty, and commitment," that, in fact, they
and the house become "one thing." At times the group
members act as one when the group is threatened or
when all work together to gain a common end. Skillfully
and calmly, under Pilon's direction, they steal delicacies
for their king, and no less skillfully but with little calm
they turn on Portagee Joe when he breaks a group oath.

Except in a few instances, however, the friendship
and loyalty of the group are not "beautiful and wise"
and their commitments are not really for each other or
the group. Only Jesus Maria, always ready to help the
cause or a stranger, and the kindly Pirate show any true
regard for others. In contrast, the chief figures, Danny
and Pilon, appear constitutionally unable to do anything
for anyone else or for the group unless they are outnum-
bered or if it is in their own interest. They are essentially
individualistic. Nor are Pablo and Portagee Joe, in their
crude ways, often outdone for self-serving tactics. Such
tactics are satirized.

In general terms, the mock-heroic satire and the pastoral sympathy are not fundamentally conflicting because to some extent Steinbeck succeeds in creating characters who possess both good and bad points and in criticizing all areas or levels of life in Monterey, not just those in the Flat.

As described in the preface, the town of Monterey consists of two parts: the lower, where "Americans, Italians, catchers and canners of fish" live; and the upper, "where the forest and town intermingle" and the paisanos live. The two parts, separated by the gulch, are seemingly as different as night and day, for, in the upper part, or the Flat, the streets are unpaved, there are no street lights, and most people "live in old wooden houses set in weedy yards." The city's businesses and small industries, located in the thriving southern half, include the Hotel Del Monico, the San Carlos Hotel, the Palace Drug Store, tailor Hugh Machado's shop, Western Warehouse, Paladine Co., the pool room on Alvarado Street, and Simon's Investment, Jewelry, and Loan Company. For entertainment, people with money can go to the Monterey Theater, the El Paseo Dancing Pavilion, or any number of bars, dancehalls, and brothels. For more routine shopping there are various stores, including the Woolworth Dime Store and the National Dollar Store.

Although in mythological terms the gulch may separate King Arthur's domain from hostile or dangerous lands, it is no hindrance in the action to anyone going north or south. Some paisanos cross and recross the gulch daily, with or without benefit. Nor does the gulch present physical or economic obstacles to the influences of one part of Monterey or the other. Although few businesses are found in the Flat, Danny and his friends operate their own businesses quite skillfully, and Torrelli loses no money in his wineshop and bootleg business.

The pastoral life, then, is not as pastoral as it appears to be. Steinbeck's statement in the preface that "the paisanos are clean of commercialism, free of the complicated systems of American business" appears to be at least partly ironic. While preferring the good simple life, Danny and friends will not work or suffer for it. To avoid such calamities and gain the essentials of the good life—wine, women, and food—they will wheel, deal, and steal with the best of them, and anywhere in Monterey. Like their economic betters, they engage in stealthy operations and explain them with high-sounding rationalizations. "Finding" a keg of nails belonging to Central Supply Co., Danny sells the nails to Western Supply for three dollars. To gain the favors of Dolores Ramerez, Danny, after some haggling, buys at Simon's for two dollars a motorless vacuum cleaner originally priced at fourteen dollars. Sometimes the round tablers do act with a minimum of selfishness, as when they steal nutritious foods for Teresina and her children and then, after the foods prove detrimental, slyly obtain the health-giving beans for them.

Danny's houses, which serve to unify and identify the group, also serve to illustrate the complex ironies of Steinbeck's treatment. Danny welcomes the status and recognition conferred by middle-class ownership, but he resents the accompanying worries that threaten his freedom. He asks his friends to pay rent, but he readily accepts gratuities instead, and gradually comes to say nothing of it. After all, rent payments and other such requirements hamper individual freedom. The unseen middle-class figures in lower Monterey who work and pay rent regularly possess little freedom. Danny and his friends, who welch on agreements and rarely work, are as free as the birds in the forest. They are, that is, until they try to act like owners and renters. They would gladly be both or either if rent-paying would produce wine and women on demand and the good life in general. But since it does not and since as realists they know that Danny will not insist on rent, they stay on in style without paying a cent. When worries of ownership grow excessive, Danny sells the remaining house to Torrelli. Although this is an acceptable middle-class maneuver, it is not acceptable to the other paisanos who, desiring the privileges of renting, proceed to destroy the evidence of the sale, a fact denied by Danny anyway. So things in the Flat continue as before until Danny dies.

The final chapter, like the preface, serves to frame the materials of *Tortilla Flat*, to link the criticism and sympathy and to present the paisanos in terms encompassing all inhabitants of the California town. In time of mourning the paisanos find themselves once again involved in middle-class conventions. Once again they are sympathetic rogues, amusing social parasites who plan to show in their own way respect for their departed leader. Middle-class conventions constrain them, however. "Imagine going to a funeral without first polishing the automobile. Imagine standing at a graveside not dressed in your best dark suit." Danny's friends have no cars and no suits, new or second-hand. There is no time to steal suits and who at such a time has a suit to lend? They must go as they are.

And that they do, standing across the street from the church, watching from the grass near the cemetery, and at the end letting the house, "This symbol of holy friendship, this good house of parties and fights, of love and comfort," burn down. They make no attempt to save the house because they prefer to see it "die as Danny died, in one last glorious, hopeless assault on the gods." Danny's boys are romantics except when they want to be something else, and often they do. The final portrait of them is critical as well as sympathetic. They are rogues, parasites, and scoundrels, who destroy private property and otherwise act in an asocial manner. But that is not so wrong in itself, for they do not want the property to fall into the wrong hands and they do not wish to act as their economic betters would act—so they walk off, toward the gulch, forest, or elsewhere, and alone.

# 3

## Conflicts and Searches
## in the 1930s

Steinbeck's remarkable versatility became evident in the
early 1930s with the publication of several of *The Long
Valley* stories, *The Pastures of Heaven,* and *Tortilla Flat.*
While his wife Carol supported them with small paychecks
from a job as typist, secretary, or editor, Steinbeck
worked steadily on other books with California backgrounds but with sharply different subject materials and
forms. What became *In Dubious Battle* (1936) was well
under way in early 1935 and depicted a California life
quite unlike that of the paisanos in peaceful Monterey in
*Tortilla Flat.* The new novel also showed unexpected
changes in form. Steinbeck's best work of the decade, with
the exception of *The Grapes of Wrath,* is *Of Mice and Men,*
published in 1937 and also in the working stage sometime
in 1935. Unlike the works already published, *In Dubious
Battle* and *Of Mice and Men* deal with economic and social
problems affecting people in California and other areas
during the Depression years.

The agricultural scene in California in the 1930s,
particularly in Salinas Valley, as Freeman Champney has
explained, differed from that of rural areas elsewhere because the California farms were large collectives, "farm
factories," owned by big operators and banks, and em-
ploying hundreds of workers, many of them migrants.[1]
Farms of a few hundred acres were comparatively
few. Although the productivity of the large farms may not

have diminished noticeably in the 1930s, low wages for picking fruit and vegetables led to economic unrest. In September 1936, thousands of lettuce workers in the Salinas Valley went on strike over low wages. The situation quickly grew tense and ominous, as Salinas officials mobilized all males in town between eighteen and forty-five and suspended civil rights for the duration. A reserve army officer was brought in to lead vigilantes against the strikers, with the result that the strike was crushed within a month. Steinbeck covered the ugly scene for the *San Francisco News*. During this time, *In Dubious Battle*, based on other strikes, was coming off the press.[2]

Steinbeck's own experiences with California farms went back to high school summers when he worked on beet ranches along the Salinas River and to the months away from Stanford when he was a straw boss and worker on the Willoughby ranch. In the winter of 1933–34, before writing *In Dubious Battle*, Steinbeck learned much about strikes and labor tactics from fugitive labor organizers, "Irish and Italian communists whose training was in the field not in the drawing room," and also, about this time, from a communist district supervisor. Information from these sources and knowledge of California strikes provided the basis for developments in the novel.[3] Steinbeck himself was not a communist and at the time was in fact critical of various communist ideas and practices, as *In Dubious Battle* makes clear. But no less than Hemingway and more than most other writers of the 1930's, Steinbeck was determined to show things as they actually are.

*In Dubious Battle* opens with scenes of Jim Nolan alone in a dingy hotel room and later with several communists. The leader, Mac, takes Jim along to Torgas Valley, where fruit workers, disgruntled over the low pay, have gone on strike. Intending to train the young man and also to impress the workers, Mac delivers the grandchild of London, a strike leader, in a tent. Later, Mac, Jim, Lon-

don, and Dakin, another leader, plan a strike against policies of the Torgas Valley Fruit Growers' Association. Mac
and Jim convince a farmer, Tom Anderson, to let fifteen
hundred to two thousand strikers camp on his land.

Learning as he goes, Jim meets Doc Burton, a non-
communist, who is in charge of sanitation and medical
care in the camp. Representatives of the growers' association quickly challenge Mac, London, and the men in an
angry confrontation. In a fierce fight in the town soon
thereafter, an old-time communist named Joy is killed.
Mac uses the death to stir up hatred. Many strikers are injured in a violent outbreak in an orchard, and Jim is shot
in the shoulder. Anger and hate mushroom on both sides.
Anderson's barn is burned down, and a grower's home is
destroyed. Jim becomes the leader, but after Doc's disappearance he is killed in an ambush. In the final scene,
with Jim's body before him, Mac speaks to the aroused
strikers.

Little in Steinbeck's previous works prepared readers
in the 1930s for the frank violence and radicalism of *In
Dubious Battle*. The battles and duels of *Cup of Gold* are
bathed in a romantic glow. A few physical attacks and
killings occur in *The Pastures of Heaven* and in *The Long
Valley*, and fights and a gang scuffle erupt in *Tortilla
Flat*. These, however, are isolated incidents that hardly
assume the proportion of homicides, beatings, and tense
confrontations in *In Dubious Battle*. Private property,
hard work, and profits are satirized in *The Pastures of
Heaven* and in *Tortilla Flat*, but radicals are not to be
found in the peaceful valley, or on either side of the gulch
in Monterey. The short story "The Raid" anticipates the
later violence and radicalism—little else does.

Such materials in the new novel proved not only different but controversial as well. Even during the Depression when strike novels were common, some readers
objected to the detailed descriptions of bloodshed and violence in *In Dubious Battle*. In commenting on such mat-

ters, one critic, Maxwell Geismar, wrote, "It seems that
. . . violence in itself has an inherent fascination for Steinbeck. . . . This violence is used for effect more than edifi-
cation." [4] As we shall see, this is not the case. There were
objections, as well, to radical ideas and tactics in the
novel. Both before and after publication, Covici and
Friede, the publishers, expressed doubts about including
such materials, and a reader for the firm ironically criticized the ideology and tactics of the radicals, suggesting
corrections and changes, all of which were subsequently
disregarded by the publisher and writer.[5] Such attitudes
are ironic in view of the fact that Steinbeck was regarded
by communists in the 1930s as "politically unreliable"
and that his novel deals as severely with radicals as with
growers.[6]

*In Dubious Battle* departs from earlier works in another respect. In general structure, it is not a collection
of stories like *The Long Valley*, an episodic novel like *The
Pastures of Heaven*, or a finely wrought comic novel like
*Tortilla Flat*. *In Dubious Battle* resembles *Tortilla Flat* in
its use of great mythical materials, including Malory's
*Morte d'Arthur* and specifically the hero Parsival, whose
family background and character—most notably his devotion to the Round Table and his chastity, as French
explains—parallel Jim's.

The dominant mythical influence, however, would appear to be Milton's *Paradise Lost*, which according to
Fontenrose's interpretation provides ironic parallels to
character and action in *In Dubious Battle*. Mac and Jim
may be regarded as satanic figures leading the party and
workers against the growers in a manner comparable to
Satan leading the Rebel Angels against Omnipotence.
The central action itself and many incidents and minor
figures, as well as names and figures of speech, gain further significance and unity through ties to materials in
*Paradise Lost*.[7] The mythic substructure enriches and
broadens the significance. As Mac and Jim realize, their

decisions and actions, and those of their opponents, have
repercussions far beyond the California borders, even
though, for the author at least, both sides are locked "in
dubious battle."

While the Miltonic parallels and ironies help determine meaning and structure in the novel, they appear less
essential than materials and patterns of labor unrest.
The abundance of these and their frank treatment
throughout identify the novel as primarily realistic and
naturalistic. *In Dubious Battle* is a proletarian work dealing with members of the working class, working class
experiences, and with conflicts between the haves and
have-nots—all essential elements in the proletarian or
radical novel. In the strict sense, however, *In Dubious
Battle* is neither, because, as Walter Rideout explains,
the one fundamental of the proletarian or radical novel
is the advocacy of Marxian ideology, and that is not to be
found in *In Dubious Battle*.[8] Yet, insofar as Marxian beliefs and practices are instrumental in the development of
plot, character, and theme, the novel has a proletarian
base. Critics express doubts, too, that *In Dubious Battle* is
a strike novel, since the emphases appear to be more on
the psychology of striker and nonstrikers than on the
strike itself.[9] This, too, is a moot point since that psychology is invariably involved with some aspect of the
strike, and most chapters deal directly or indirectly with
confrontations in Torgas Valley between strikers and nonstrikers. Steinbeck's novel may be unique in managing to
combine dramatizations of internal and external stresses
without overemphasizing the external and particularly
the violent.

Giving shape to the various materials of *In Dubious
Battle* is the plot itself: this is not plot in the simplistic or
mechanical sense but plot in the sense of the fusion of the
literal action on the one hand and the underlying causes
and thematic designs of that action on the other hand.
These causes and motives may have their origins in the

circumstances—in this case, the situation in Torgas Valley, the strike itself; in the characters' attitudes; and in their beliefs of long-term ideas. While plot in the novel hardly possesses the solidity of a Jamesian plot or the intricacy of a Faulknerian plot, it is effectively unified and things move forward in a generally necessary and probable fashion.

Essential to this progression and the novel's unity are fundamental ideas, usually political or economic, advanced by the major characters and a few minor ones. If *In Dubious Battle* is not a proletarian novel of ideas, it is a Depression strike novel with proletarian elements and powerfully influenced by specific beliefs and ideas. A few aspects of this view of the novel can be noted through comment on sequences of chapters.

Although the opening chapters include no abstract discussions or heady arguments, Mac and Jim clarify several basic ideas in early scenes. Jim is the first to discuss the relationship of anger and violence—an important relationship throughout. His own sense of anger grew out of an unhappy, insecure home life and subsequent hardships. Feeling "dead" and without purpose, Jim has sought for answers or guidance in works by Plato, Herodotus, Kant, and others, including Edward Bellamy. Although neither an intellectual nor, later, a thinking man's communist, Jim is intelligent and reflective and in many ways a student. He learns from Harry Nilson, a party official, of the party's two punishments, and at least listens to Joy's rudimentary explanations of capitalist ideology. Mac, who expresses contempt for ideas, nonetheless insists on the importance of a few: the value of experiences—books are of little help, he explains; the necessity of violence—fighting unifies strikers and a death can anger them; and the need to take the long view and to be objective. The last two points reappear in Doc's discussions. In a few days Jim proves himself to be an apt student both of ideas and practical experience.

The teacher-student relationship continues in chapters 4–7 as Mac demonstrates ideas in action. He shows his pragmatic bent in Torgas Valley by delivering Lisa's baby. Sometimes, the idea or theory precedes practice, as Mac reveals in talking with Jim afterwards:

You acted sure enough, Jim said.

Well, Christ Almighty, I had to! We've got to use whatever material comes to us. That was a lucky break. We simply had to take it. Course it was nice to help the girl, but hell, even if it killed her—we've got to use anything.

Although seemingly callous, Mac is not essentially so; nor does he want to be. But, as the end justifies the means, an individual may have to be sacrificed for the end or cause. Similarly, Mac believes that "there's just one rule—use whatever material you've got."

During this time of apprenticeship, Jim learns of related rules: leadership in the field must come from the men, in this instance chiefly London; workers can be taught and they like to work together. That such ideas have consequences is evident later, as Anderson, after listening to Mac's explanation of town economics, agrees to let the strikers camp on his land. The lesson is reaffirmed in the camp, as Mac clarifies, if simplistically, essentials of the confrontation in Torgas: one side has money and guns; his side has neither. As the two sides meet in chapter 7, the exchange is not of ideas but of threats and counterthreats with violence only a step or shout away. The scene dramatizes the likely effects of ideas and ways of life advocated by men who will countenance only their own ways of thinking or doing things.

The inevitable consequences of irreconcilable viewpoints appear in chapters 8–12 as violence erupts. Scenes of violence are roughly alternated with scenes of argument and discussion. The dominant speakers are Mac and Doc Burton. Doc introduces the third ideology in the

novel, the other two being communism and capitalism.
Doc, a medical scientist, is the first serious exponent in
Steinbeck's fiction of "is-thinking." Whereas Mac draws
from communist experiences and Jim from these and
other experiences and from reading, Doc turns naturally
to science for explanations and analogies. He tells Mac:

I want to watch these group-men, for they seem to me to be
a new individual, not at all like single men. A man in a
group isn't himself at all, he's a cell in an organism that
isn't like him any more than the cells in your body are like
you. I want to watch the group, and see what it's like.

The emphasis in Doc's approach is upon facts, processes,
and objectivity, upon studying things or men as they
actually are and as they appear and behave in a group.
While Doc wants to see the "whole picture," he does not
believe in beginnings or endings, nor in applying ethical
judgments. Strikes are not "good" or "bad"; they are just
like body infections or processes that must be studied and
understood.

The teleological thinking of Mac and Jim, which
makes moral judgements and looks for beginnings and
endings, is regarded by Doc as unsound. He finds in Jim's
devotion to the cause a religious intensity, and he tells
Mac, "You're the craziest mess of cruelty and hausfrau
sentimentality, of clear vision and rose-colored glasses I
ever saw." While admiring the doctor's knowledge and
intelligence, Mac and Jim ironically regard him not as essentially objective, but as essentially unrealistic.

The three major ideologies are dramatized in chapters 13–15, beginning with the appearance of Bolter, the
newly elected president of the Fruit Growers' Association.
Pleasant and composed, Bolter speaks in idealized, abstract terms of America, the working man, cooperation
of labor and capital, and money and profit. He believes
that it is reasonable to ask working men to return to work

if both growers and strikers are losing money—to accept
first twenty cents per hour and then one-half of the de-
manded hourly increase. The offer and his version of economic facts are bitterly derided by Mac in particular,
who gives his own version of the facts, exclaiming "I'm
not talkin' right and wrong now, mister. I'm tellin' you
what happens." Threats of force will likely lead to violence. The scene that follows—of Jim and Doc arguing
about ends—illustrates the fundamental contrast of the
teleological and the nonteleological.

In remaining scenes Mac appears more resilient than
Jim. Mac survives because he can manipulate ideas and at
the same time not lose sight of people and facts. Doc dies
because he is a good man who allows a conception of reality to disguise or hide threats and dangers in others. Because his sense of mission and religious ecstasy blinds him
to the facts, Jim cannot survive as the new leader.

In creating Depression figures and controversies,
Steinbeck relied upon several techniques, including a
third-person point of view that minimizes the writer's
preferences and concentrates on the facts or appearances
of a scene or incident. What has been called "middle distance" is appropriate in creating down-to-earth characters who belong in a 1930s strike scene. Harry Nilson's
wary alertness, his concentration, are suggested in his intense eyes and in heavy facial lines. Mac's appearance
and mannerisms give a sense of physical strength and
dedication. The stress throughout on physical qualities and
mannerisms creates at times an almost palpable sense of
tension. Mac has obviously been around: he is tough and
smart, ready to act, talk, do whatever is necessary. Jim
is honest and alert, buffeted a little by experience but possessing the grit and stamina to keep up with Mac.

Because of the middle-distance stance, scenes of
Mac, Jim, and others are frequent and contribute to the
sense of the present. The overall development reflects a

similar objectivity and directness: in the general lack of authorial commentary and restricted uses of description and explanation; in the careful proportioning of chapters; and in the proportional relating of personal and crowd scenes, of talk or peaceful activity, and of tense or violent situations.

To create such characters and scenes of the 1930s, Steinbeck relied upon appropriate—that is, recognizable —everyday language and dialogue. The speech had to be idiomatic and natural as well as commonplace. Accordingly, characters in the novel use slang, awkward or fragmented expressions, and invective; they pronounce the final g or drop it, depending upon the occasion, for, as Steinbeck explained in a letter to his publisher, that was how the language was actually spoken.[10]

A preoccupation with verisimilitude is evident also in descriptive passages of the novel. A grim Depression scene is suggested in a brief account of a group of workers:

An apathy had fallen on the men. They sat staring in front of them. They seemed not to have the energy to talk, and among them the bedraggled, discontented women sat. They were listless and stale. They gnawed thoughtfully at their meat, and when it was finished, wiped their hands on their clothes.

The prose is equal to more complex demands: figures of speech suggest an ironic parallel to something in Malory or Milton: poetic rhythms create a peaceful or dreamlike state in the midst of a strike.

Several other techniques are used to advantage. Contrast is a factor on different levels: the general one of opposition between the haves and the have-nots, between opposing ideologies, and, more dramatically, in the pairing of unlike figures: Mac and Jim, Mac and Doc, the two Andersons, old Dan and Jim, and Bolter and a strike

leader. The group-man configuration is a technique or pattern in portrayals of strikers and nonstrikers alike. Another is the use of Doc Burton as a chorus figure to provide commentary on ideas or action. The use of clearly
allegorical figures like Joy, the super, the sheriff, and
others is designed to illustrate views of one side or the
other and also the inevitability of opposition and violence.

Weaknesses or limitations in *In Dubious Battle* tend
to be excesses of strong points. Several can be noted.
While the middle distance stance and objectivity contribute to realistic speech, manners, and appearance, they
restrict characterizations, stop short of psychological
probing—a tendency evident in Steinbeck's earlier fiction. When this is coupled with an emphasis upon ideas
and mythical elements, a character's motivations or feelings may be glossed over. He may become an allegorical
figure in a generally realistic context, as happens in *In
Dubious Battle*. For example, Mac, an effective im-
promptu speaker, in moments of anger appears grotesque
or satanic; his underlying feelings remain vague. London's strength and honesty make him a natural leader,
but descriptions of his musculature make him at such
times inhuman, or, on one level, a 1930s Beelzebub. At
such times both figures are unconvincing abstractions. In
the late chapters, the nature of Jim's maturation as a
leader and of Mac's growing weariness are only vaguely
clarified by such allegorical emphases.

The sense of unrealness detracts from Steinbeck's
overall treatment of key characters and issues. The emphasis furthermore, contributes to a certain bareness in
the development. Foreshadowing is at times too obvious;
Dakin's pride in his truck indicates a likely loss of both
owner and truck; Dan's boasting in one scene foretells
trouble for him in a subsequent scene. Discussions of
ideas, with some exceptions, appear simplified, as if the
writer could not be bothered with complications. The prose
style itself is sometimes a little too bare and unadorned

All this is to say that the novel is generally sound but hardly brilliant.

The much shorter *Of Mice and Men* begins on a Salinas River bank as two men—George Milton, small and alert, and Lennie, his powerful and retarded friend —talk about their dream of a farm of their own. The next morning, reporting for work at a ranch, they meet Candy, an old disabled swamper, the boss, the boss's arrogant son, Curley, and Curley's wife, a cheaply pretty woman whom George immediately recognizes as trouble. That night in the bunkhouse George tells Slim, the skinner, of Lennie's background and his trouble in Weed, a previous stop. Later, after George recounts the dream to Lennie and an interested Candy, Curley starts a fight with Lennie, who crushes his hand. On Saturday night, while others are in town, Lennie, Candy, and Crooks, the black stable worker, talk until Curley's wife interrupts them and they disperse. On Sunday afternoon, alone in the barn, Lennie accidentally kills first a puppy and then the lonely wife, who had wanted to be friendly. Later that afternoon, as everyone else searches for Lennie, George finds him on the river bank. He has no choice but to shoot him. Afterwards George walks off with Slim.

*Of Mice and Men* and *In Dubious Battle* differ in that the former lacks widespread violence, class conflict, and Marxian ideology. They are similar in that the characters have working-class backgrounds and the story is set on large California ranches during the Depression. Conditions in *Of Mice and Men* do appear less grim, but they are hardly reassuring or normal. Men must go from ranch to ranch to work for their "50 and found." Lennie and George, who find a place through "Murray and Ready's," an employment agency of some kind, are treated like numbers: they receive work slips and bus tickets. Like others they carry their few possessions in a blanket, or "bindle," and are called "bindle stiffs" by Curley's wife.

The fifty-dollar salary does not last long, for, as George confesses only too sadly, it can disappear in a Saturday night in town, the only genuine relief from the monotony of farm work. So the men keep moving, and most with no hope whatsoever. As George explains to both himself and sidekick Lennie,

Guys like us, that work on ranches, are the loneliest guys in the world. They got no family. They don't belong no place. They . . . work up a stake and . . . blow their stake, and the first thing you know they're poundin' their tail on some other ranch. They ain't got nothing to look ahead to.

But in this novel of hard knocks and low pay, characters have a few things to look forward to. A man can usually find work at fifty dollars per month, plus room and board, which is better than the fifteen or twenty cents per hour the strikers in Torgas Valley might receive. If a migrant is steady and reliable, he could possibly stay on indefinitely at a ranch. His search for security could end there as it has for Carlson, who can put in eleven hours daily bucking barley and worry about nothing. Of course, like others Carlson has nothing to dream about, either. Another possibility, realized by few, is represented by Slim, the jerkline skinner, "capable of driving ten, sixteen, even twenty mules with a single line to the leaders." Among ranch workers Slim has reached the top. He has unusual skill with wagons and mules, knows all phases of ranch work, and is the acknowledged leader wherever he may be. Having no conflict or doubts, Slim is not looking for something better. He seemingly has no dreams.

The dream itself is the final possibility. This is not the elaborate communist dream of Mac and Jim in *In Dubious Battle*, but the personal, limited dream of two drifters like George and Lennie.[11] One essential for such a dream, particularly its realization, is friendship, and that too must be of a special kind. There are friendships on the ranch—of Slim and Carlson, Candy and Crooks—but these are either temporary or ordinary. The friendship of George and Lennie, which goes back many years, is based on various needs. The mentally retarded Lennie, who cannot survive on his own, needs the protection and guidance of someone like George. Without George, Lennie would run off to a cave in the hills, as he sometimes threatens to do, or find himself in an institution. The comparatively self-sufficient George complains regularly about Lennie's stupidity and helplessness. Complaining can take the edge off the monotony and loneliness of ranch life; it can also enhance his sense of superiority. But afterwards George feels guilty about getting angry at Lennie, and he feels also a grudging affection that he would not openly admit. Lennie in turn has come to love the person who is all things to him.

Without the friendship, neither George nor Lennie could sustain a dream, let alone realize its fulfillment. With the friendship, the dream becomes a possibility. That the possibility is remote is suggested by dramatic ironies of the action from the beginning. There are many obstacles. But early and middle scenes of the novel indicate also that the two men have a chance. George is intelligent, experienced, and capable of managing a farm. Lennie is tractable and possesses the strength to do much of the farm work. And since the farm exists and has a price of six hundred dollars, George's articulate description of it makes it real:

Well, it's ten acres. . . . Got a little win'mill. Got a little shack on it, an' a chicken run. Got a kitchen, orchard, cherries, apples, peaches, 'cots, nuts, got a few berries. They's a place for alfalfa and plenty water to flood it. They's a pig pen.

An' rabbits, George.

No place for rabbits now, but I could easy build a few hutches and you could feed alfalfa to the rabbits.

As George talks on, he becomes entranced with his own picture of the simple pastoral life with each doing his part and all of them living, as Lennie says, "off the fatta the lan'." Yet George admits that he and Lennie have only ten dollars between them. When Candy eagerly offers to put in three hundred and fifty dollars of his own, prospects immediately brighten. Candy would contribute to both friendship and dream.

Yet the dramatic ironies and the facts of life prevail in *Of Mice and Men*. The dream cannot continue and the friendship is destroyed. With his predilection for accidental violence, Lennie kills Curley's wife and in turn is killed by George. Both the men and their dream are defeated by circumstances, by chance, by "something that happened," Steinbeck's first title for the book. The final title of the novel, selected from the familiar line of poet Robert Burns, "The best laid schemes o' mice an' men Gang aft a-gley," is more specific and pessimistic.[12] The handicapped in the migrant world—the Lennies, Candys, and Crookes—are doomed or fated. The Georges just manage to get by, to wander off down the road. With the dream George was a better man, or capable of being one. With Lennie gone, that possibility and the dream are gone forever.

In portraying dreams, friendships, and grim necessities, Steinbeck wrote his best novel to date. A more sensitive and perceptive work than *Tortilla Flat* or *In Dubious Battle*, *Of Mice and Men* compares favorably with the best short novels of the decade. It is also the first and best of Steinbeck's experiments with the novel-play form, which combines qualities of each genre. Well-received as a novel in early 1937, *Of Mice and Men* needed few changes before appearing on stage in November as a prize-winning play. The novel version shows an essentially play form. The six chapters can be regarded as comprising three acts of two chapters each. The individual chapters or scenes contain few descriptions of place, character, or action. The unities in *Of Mice and Men* are based on drastic limitations. Action is restricted usually to the bunkhouse. The restriction of time to three days—sunset Thursday to sunset Sunday—intensifies suspense and drama. With place and time compressed, the action is necessarily simple and dramatic; the superfluous and complex have been eliminated. There are no scenes of travel or of work and few of the past. Foreshadowing is obvious and suspenseful. Lennie's rough play with mice and the shooting of Candy's old dog foretell subsequent violence. Future action is more or less anticipated by what is said. And the characters themselves make for simplicity of action.

To create such effects, Steinbeck's craftsmanship was at its best. All aspects of the novel are finely done. A few techniques can be noted. A general technique, as the above would suggest, is a highly restricted focus. With the emphasis upon the scenic, a skillfully managed third-person point of view is also essential. To create a sense of the impersonal and objective, Steinbeck concentrates, with exceptions, on exteriors: a river bank, a bunkhouse, a character's appearance, card players at a table. The setting is not panoramic, as in the description of a valley scene in *In Dubious Battle;* it is, figuratively speaking, only as wide as a stage. The focus is also upon the present: what can be seen or heard. Thoughts, recollections, and fantasies are directly expressed by the characters involved, except in the case of Lennie's Aunt Clara and the giant rabbit in chapter 6. This interlude of fantasy may or may not violate the objectivity of the third-person narration. Generally, however, the point of view remains objective and exterior.

The prose style—particularly the rhythms and diction—possess greater sensitivity and naturalness than in *In Dubious Battle.* The language is generally more realistic and precise. Descriptions of the bunkhouse interior— walls, bunks, scanty possessions, stove and table, George's things—and of sights and sounds in Crooks's room and the barn, create a sense of the workaday world and its

crudities. Hanging in the harness room, where Crooks
stays, are "pieces of harness, a split collar with the horse-
hair stuffing sticking out, a broken hame, and a trace chain
with its leather covering split." The precision is notable.
Although there are no work scenes, references to bucking
barley eleven hours daily, to workers who put in a month
and leave, to evenings of card games and pulp magazines underline the weary monotony. The physical bareness of the bunkhouse, the mechanical neatness of bunks
and wooden boxes, suggest a bareness of spirit as well.
Yet, appearing throughout the novel, often in ironic contrast, are sensitive, sometimes poetic descriptions of the
pleasant, secure, or beautiful: the pastoral scene at the
beginning; the warm, sunlit scene in the barn on early
Sunday afternoon; the late afternoon scene at the "green
pool of the Salinas River" at the end.

The symbolism, which does not include the pervasive
mythical materials of *In Dubious Battle,* is convincingly
part of the talk, places, and incidents of the time. The
river bank scene is at least suggestive of life-in-nature,
a level Lennie is not too far above. The river bank is
reassuringly peaceful until George fires the luger and
destroys friend and dream. The ranch provides another
kind of security and also a place for dreams; but for the
Lennies and the Georges of the world it remains essentially unfulfilling.

The river bank and the ranch provide on one level
the idyllic and real boundaries of their world. The cen-
trally placed bunkhouse and barn, offering only physical
security and a minimum of that, symbolize the essential
emptiness and impersonality of that world. The fundamental symbol is the dream itself—"a little house and a
couple of acres an' a cow and some pigs and . . ."—
which keeps the two men together, stimulates hopes for
two others, and very likely expresses the hopes of still
others. (The "little house" symbol reappears under more
difficult circumstances in *The Grapes of Wrath.*) The ac-

tion traced in *Of Mice and Men,* possessing a parable-like simplicity and theme, reminds one of journeys of other figures in American fiction, Wellingborough Redburn, Huck Finn, and Henry Fleming, who with others also search for ever-elusive goals.

Another mark of excellence appears in the variety and depth of characterization. Although considered by some critics as subhuman, Lennie is more like an over-grown, retarded boy capable of hope and love. His potentiality for violence is instinctual but motivated primarily by innocence and childish possessiveness. He must pet and pacify living things. George complements Lennie's sheer corporality with his own quickness. He is shrewdly adaptable, alert to the nitty-gritty of migratory life. However, George has his weaknesses: he carps at Lennie, needs him to feel better about his own ordinariness, and tends to drift. But the man is essentially sound. He finally admits the dream would not have worked out, and he possesses the courage and common sense to lie about the shooting of Lennie. Candy and Crooks are very credibly drawn victims of age, economic pressures, or racial prejudice, and they illustrate the technique of creating complementary figures. Crooks's bitter dignity and frankness illustrate also Steinbeck's own frank criticisms of society's failures in the 1930s, but Crooks is his own man and not a cardboard figure speaking for the author. The swaggering Curley is somewhat stereotyped; his unnamed wife, however, is not a "tart," as she is described by several characters, but a victim of a shallow, selfish imagination. Her pathetic loneliness and dream of movie stardom reflect the monotony of ranch life and her own doom. The superb dialogue gives life to all the characters.

In the last analysis, George and Lennie symbolize something of the enduring and hopeful as well as the meaningless. They manage—if only for a brief time—to rise above circumstances and to convince others as well as themselves that dreams are part of the territory, that all they have to do is keep working and hoping and some day they will have their own place. If they could only somehow control their own weaknesses and keep a little ahead of circumstances. But they cannot. These and other matters are examined by Steinbeck in more complex terms and with greater range and authority in *The Grapes of Wrath*.

# 4

# Affirmation and Protest
# in the West

With little fanfare and only one public announcement a few months before, Steinbeck's eighth work was published 14 March 1939. A reading public already impressed with the merits of *In Dubious Battle* and *Of Mice and Men* was waiting. *The Grapes of Wrath* sold at the rate of 2500 copies daily shortly after its appearance, reached the top of the best-seller list by 6 May, and remained there throughout the year, with some 430,000 copies printed. In 1940 *The Grapes of Wrath* proved so popular that when the movie version starring Henry Fonda and John Carradine came out that year no special edition was necessary. The novel has been continuously in print since then, appearing in both expensive illustrated editions and paperbacks, and in French, German, and Japanese translations.[1] As an American classic of the 1930s and a familiar title on college reading lists, *The Grapes of Wrath* has been read by many thousands of students since the end of World War II.

Several factors likely accounted for the novel's original popularity and recognition. The Depression was by no means over in 1939, and many readers found in *The Grapes of Wrath* a frank portrayal of drought and migrant problems which they had read about in newspapers and may have been involved in themselves. The price of $2.75, moreover, was not excessive for a novel that was itself in the news. Newspaper and radio accounts of reactions in Oklahoma and California to *The Grapes of Wrath* no doubt helped sell many copies. Civic and agricultural groups attacked what they regarded as gross distortions of conditions in the 1930s. Governors and other high state officials in the two states, not to mention numerous editors, tried to make clear to the public that many things in the novel were simply not true. Reactions elsewhere in the country added to the controversy. The novel was banned by several libraries and school boards, national columnists Westbrook Pegler and Raymond Clapper denounced aspects of it, and an editorial in *Collier's*, a national weekly, condemned it as communistic propaganda.[2]

The sensational reception of *The Grapes of Wrath* may have been due also to the inclusion of four-letter words and sexual allusions in a day when their presence in print was not common; realistic portrayals of typical characters and situations; controversial social and religious views. Readers and reviewers interested in the novel as literature and not as sociology were generally impressed. For the editor of *The Atlantic Monthly*, Edward Weeks, *The Grapes of Wrath* was "the summation of eighteen years of realism" and "essentially a healthy and disciplined work of art." Joseph Henry Jackson, novelist and critic, writing in the *New York Herald Tribune*, found the novel to be profoundly sincere and truthful and an outstanding creative effort on any level.[3] The novel was clearly superior to Steinbeck's earlier works, several steps in quality above *Gone With the Wind*, another widely read novel of the day, and as remarkable a book as Hemingway's *For Whom the Bell Tolls*, which appeared in 1940. Most critics polled by the *Saturday Review of Literature* in 1940 supported the magazine in nominating *The Grapes of Wrath* as the most distinguished novel of the year. Shortly thereafter, Steinbeck received the Pulitzer Prize for 1940.[4]

Appearing in a decade that saw the publication also of *As I Lay Dying* and *Absalom, Absalom!* by William Faulkner and the trilogy *USA* by John Dos Passos, *The Grapes of Wrath* is one of the period's brilliant, innovative works. It combines a long, eventful narrative and many passages of exposition, broadens the narrative level with several important structural patterns, and demonstrates, among other things, the writer's imaginative techniques and craftsmanship. Highlights of the narrative can be noted first.

After release from an Oklahoma state prison, Tom Joad heads for home, meets Jim Casy on the way, and discovers that his family, having lost both land and home, is packing to move to California. After accepting Casy into the family, the Joads, unified around the parents and particularly around Ma Joad, depart on the loaded-down Hudson Super Six. Early in the journey, Grandpa Joad dies; he is buried with the aid of the Wilsons, a Kansas couple. At various places along Highway 66, the Joads encounter suspicious and hostile natives, others going west, and warnings that California will prove disappointing. At the Colorado River the Wilsons and Noah, another son, leave the group, and the ailing grandmother dies as the Joads cross the Mojave Desert. At the deplorable Hooverville camp, the family's first lengthy stop, Jim goes to jail to save Tom, and Rose of Sharon's husband, Connie, deserts. Ma Joad's strength and determination keep the family going. The Joads stay next at the pleasant Weedpatch camp, but leave to work in the Hooper orchard, unaware that it is under strike and that Casy, out of jail, is the strike leader. When he is struck down, Tom kills the man. The Joads flee north, find a camp of railroad boxcars and tents, work and eat regularly, as Tom hides out in a cave nearby. After Ruthie carelessly reveals his whereabouts, Ma tells Tom that he must leave. Later, during a flood, Rose of Sharon has a stillbirth. Afterwards, the remaining Joads flee to a barn, where, to save a starving man, the young woman nurses him at her breast.

Several structural levels are suggested in this summary. A prominent mythical level, more concretely developed than those in *Tortilla Flat* and *In Dubious Battle*, is the biblical. The journey of the twelve Joads resembles that of the twelve tribes of Israel in the Old Testament. Like the Jews in Egypt under Pharaoh, the Joads in Oklahoma are oppressed by landowners and banks. When dust, drought, and oppression prove to be too much, the Joads begin their exodus and years of wandering. Like the ancient Jews, the Joads must face down detractors and enemies to reach California, or Canaan, "the promised land." There they must remain off the land unless the growers need them for work. Besides this general narrative pattern, a wealth of specific biblical materials has been described by Fontenrose and others. Many characters possess biblical names, identities, or ties. Jim Casy, a Christ-like figure, is himself a leader of a new religion. Tom possesses qualities of both Peter and Moses. Noah, Rose of Sharon, and John suggest biblical counterparts, and Connie may be regarded as a Judas. Various activities involving the Joads and others carry universal significance because such biblical overtones and associations add depth to accounts of the 1930s.[5]

The biblical level represents an ancient epical tradition, but the novel is also an epic of modern times, for, like Faulkner's Bundrens in *As I Lay Dying*, the Joads must survive trials by fire, drought, and flood, and, as a simple rural people, they must deal also with death and birth. In their determination and pride, the Joads celebrate qualities of the common man, and their leaders show remarkable courage in coping with obstacles and enemies.

In contrast to the epical characteristics, the equally important naturalistic level reflects pessimistic and deterministic elements in the novel. Driven from the land by economic and natural forces they cannot control or moderate, the Joads remain vulnerable during their journey. They cannot save the grandparents, survive alone, or prevent Noah's disappearance. In California, work, money, and security prove scarce. In the end, despite tenacity and hard work, the remaining Joads appear to be all but defeated.

To create a work of such scope and depth, Steinbeck relied upon a number of techniques. The most general one pertains to the language itself, which, in order to serve various functions, had to be supple and figurative, yet often plain. The novel has in fact several languages. There is, for example, a documentary prose for information on states, towns, and highways in the western United States. There is a blunt, straightforward language to convey a sense of the impersonal or inhumane owners and bank-manipulated forces. For descriptions of corrupt business practices, the prose rhythms speed up, words grow shrill or metallic. A more poetic and ironic prose describes the ripe beauty of California fruit and vegetables likely to rot while people go hungry. A similarly graceful and firm prose describes the Oklahoma countryside, while the earthy and idiomatic speech of the Joads and others is presented accurately. These various levels of language, both written and spoken, show affinities with the free verse of Whitman and Sandburg, the ironic simplicity of Hemingway, and the distinctive rhythm and phrasing of biblical passages.[6] The most characteristic qualities of the written language are precision, natural and sometimes biblical rhythms, and imagery customarily based on elements of the land or daily life.

Craftsmanship in *The Grapes of Wrath* is generally excellent in other respects as well. While customarily narrated in the third-person voice, the novel's point of view varies dramatically in tone, purpose, and method, providing an elevated panoramic view, as in most intercalary chapters, or a close dramatic one, as in narrative chapters. The point of view within a chapter, moreover, may shift from the personal to the impersonal, from the objective to the ironic. Steinbeck's skillful use of point of view and related techniques can be illustrated in terms of a distinctive feature of the novel—the intercalary chapters.

These sixteen chapters, usually the odd-numbered ones, provide social and historical background for the experiences of the Joads and others in the mid-1930s. The background may range from descriptions of agricultural conditions in Oklahoma (chapter 1); to accounts of highways and roads west from Arkansas and Oklahoma (chapter 12); to information on California's origin and land ownership (chapter 19). Such chapters, illuminating basic themes of land and conflict, often include narrative sections and scenes dramatizing such themes. More restricted chapters are directly related to predicaments of the Joads. Chapter 5, which explains and dramatizes the economic conflict of tenants and landowners, includes a scene of a bitter encounter between a tractor operator and a tenant family to be evicted. Consisting almost entirely of the sales pitch of a used-car dealer, chapter 7 presents a scene very likely familiar to Al and father Tom. Chapter 9 employs the technique of an anonymous narrator selling family possessions and thinking bitterly of what they represent. The brilliant chapter 15 is in effect a short story portraying a typical hamburger stand and signs of the 1930s: a weary waitress and cook, a needy tenant family, and a flabby couple with money. Most of the intercalary chapters develop basic symbols of the novel: land, family, the clash between the haves and have-nots. The land turtle, introduced in chapter 3 and reappearing thereafter, symbolizes qualities of the Joads and also of the persevering Jim Casy.

These various symbols and themes help unify the different materials and to relate intercalary and narrative chapters. References to grapes and vineyards, with their biblical and economic connotations, appear throughout the novel, as do also images of money, dust, animals, and vehicles.[7] References to the Joads and other families, to the land, to a familiar action clarify and relate materials. Most chapters create a sense of movement in space: to the west or, in California, to the next camp. They also suggest a movement in time: from the usually reassuring past to the difficult present, to the end of a day, a harvest, someone's life.

Because of the novel's scope and complexity, discussion will be limited primarily to several major topics: to aspects of territory, family, and journey, and to themes of conflict, protest, and affirmation. The order of discussion will follow the three main sequences of action: the Joads in Oklahoma, chapters 1–11; their journey, chapters 12–18; and the Joads in California, chapters 19–30.

Although Steinbeck's *East of Eden* (1952) covers greater expanses of the country than does *The Grapes of Wrath*, descriptions in the former of land outside California are somewhat sketchy. The territory of *The Grapes of Wrath* is, by most comparisons, vast, and much of it is described in detail. The territory includes most of Oklahoma, portions of other states, and a large area of California. The novel begins appropriately with descriptions of Oklahoma land, presumably in the mid-1930s:

To the red country and part of the gray country of Oklahoma, the last rains came gently, and they did not cut the scarred earth. . . . The last rains lifted the corn quickly and scattered weed colonies and grass along the sides of the roads. . . . In the last part of May the sky grew pale and the clouds that had hung in high puffs for so long in the spring were dissipated. The sun flared down on the growing corn day after day. . . . The surface of the earth crusted, a thin hard crust. . . . Then it was June, and the sun shone more fiercely.

As heat and dryness continue through the summer, crops gradually dry up and a fine dust fills the air. The region becomes a midwest wasteland. Effects of the drought are described in intercalary chapters 5 and 11, as owners argue over the dying land and farmlands and buildings are left vacant. The panoramic scene is a fictional reproduction of dust-bowl conditions in the 1930s, when for many farmers in Oklahoma and in nearby states parched earth and swirling clouds of dust were daily facts of life.

The early narrative chapters focus on land near Sallisaw, in the east-central part of Oklahoma. The land is a far cry in richness or fertility from that of ranches in Salinas Valley. Yet in good years, a farmer can earn enough from raising corn or cotton to provide adequately for his family and feel a sense of identity, if not of ownership. Most farmers in that area and surrounding ones are sharecroppers, that is, small farmers, who may have owned the land at one time but lost it and must rent the land and share crop proceeds with the landlord, bank, or other lending agency. In poor years, the farmer has to borrow heavily in order to make the payments. When that cannot be done, the land is sold or rented to someone else. When the land is lost, the farmer loses not only the source of income but, as *The Grapes of Wrath* makes poignantly clear, an identity and a way of life.

The principal focus in early and later chapters, however, is not so much on the land as on the farmers themselves and their families. In a general sense *The Grapes of Wrath* is a book about families. These include the many anonymous families appearing throughout the novel, usually in intercalary chapters; the individual families, particularly the Joads and a few others; and, in a general or thematic sense, the family of men.

The anonymous families described in the early chapters are Oklahoma families, unidentified sharecroppers caught in the drought. Accounts of them are impersonal, almost documentary—a fictional reportage describing the situations of thousands. In chapter 1 the word "family" does not appear. The anonymous families are identified as "men and women," "they," "the people," who,

lying in their beds, heard the wind stop. They awakened when the rushing wind was gone. They lay quietly. . . . The people came out of their houses and smelled the hot stinging air and covered their noses from it. . . . Men stood by their fences and looked at the ruined corn. . . . After a while the faces of the watching men . . . became hard and angry and resistant. Then the women knew that they were safe and that there was no break.

Families remain steadfast in the early chapters even though many are entangled in economic processes far more predictable than nature's cycles and at times no less devastating.

The views and feelings of dispossessed families are particularized in accounts of the Joads, Steinbeck's most significant family and as noteworthy in modern American fiction as Cather's Bergsons and Faulkner's Bundrens. In early chapters, the Joads, despite losses, appear realistic and hardworking. They come by both traits naturally, for they have learned to make do with what they have. The grandfather's full name, William James Joad, with its implied reference to the American philosopher, suggests the preoccupation with the facts, things, and consequences of everyday life. That the Oklahoma prairie pragmatism is conditioned somewhat by the family's Protestant fundamentalism is evident in references to Jim Casy's ministry, old and new, to emotional responses of the Joads to prayer or revival, and to the importance of the Bible as a literal transcription of God's word. Yet only John Joad is troubled by a strong sense of sin and guilt, and the grandparents have grown fuzzy-minded about Bible teachings. The parents take their religion realistically, with no feelings of superiority or intolerance. For Ma Joad, belief in God means a belief in love, patience, and tolerance.

The Joads manage to stay together for many months. Their sense of unity, which is based on mutual depen- dence, tolerance, and grudging affection, is long stand- ing. The sharecropping life has required that each one pitch in and do his or her share. Before marriage and pregnancy, Rose of Sharon no doubt helped her mother with household chores. The small children had chores to do and in busy times other things as well. When not chasing girls, Al worked with his father around the barn and in the field. With the farm gone, everyone continues to do his or her share. The parents have always worked the longest hours and serve as examples in other respects as well. They appear fair in their expectations of others, and, while not emotional or demonstrative, Ma and Pa Joad leave no doubt as to their affection for the children. Young and old share a sense of pride in the family.

Appearing in the pages of *The Grapes of Wrath* are many characters, some of them unforgettable. The Joads are impressively drawn: a down-to-earth farm family un- exceptional in most respects but determined to survive and keep their identities intact. Ma Joad, the central figure, is very likely the most memorable in Steinbeck's fiction. A person of common sense, stamina, and compassion, Ma symbolizes both the family's strength and the eternal qualities of motherhood. She is a pioneering woman brought to life in Oklahoma in the 1930s. Upon his return, Tom sees her for the first time in the kitchen:

Ma was heavy, but not fat; thick with child-bearing and work. She wore a loose Mother Hubbard of gray cloth . . . which . . . came down to her ankles. . . . Her thin, steel- gray hair was gathered in a sparse wispy knot at the back of her head. Strong, freckled arms were bare to the elbow, and her hands were chubby and delicate, like those of a plump little girl. . . . Her hazel eyes seemed to have experienced all possible tragedy and . . . suffering like steps into a high calm and a superhuman understanding.

The description continues with statements of praise that tend to sentimentalize the portrait by emphasizing ideas or ideals at the expense of characterization. The descriptions testify not only to Steinbeck's compassion and idealism but also to a temporary failure to make the symbolism believable. Generally Ma Joad's physical presence, her speech and manner, make her credible and also illustrate her excellent but still very human qualities.[8]

The novel's most vital characters after Ma Joad are Tom and Jim Casy. After four years in McAlester State Prison, Tom appears wary, matter-of-fact, and quietly confident. Fortunately, he has developed his mother's ability to learn as he goes along, a crucial capacity in unpredictable Depression times. A shrewd judge of character, Tom likes the talkative, usually mild preacher. The preacher comes from another prison—that of his earlier Christian fundamentalism with its undercurrents of sexuality. Putting behind him both fundamentalism and sexuality, Jim is ready for a new life. He is honest, compassionate, and courageously dedicated to helping people like the Joads.

The talk of Tom and Jim on the country road illustrates Steinbeck's advances in dramatizing ideas since *In Dubious Battle*. The road scene has little of the classroom aura evident in the earlier novel. Although the scene involves less an exchange of ideas than an interrupted monologue by Jim, the explanations and Tom's remarks are frank and spoken in the dry June heat. Doc Burton in *In Dubious Battle* advocates a scientific pragmatism; Jim presents here a down-home blend of common sense and non-Christian American ethics. Explaining that there is no sin or virtue, he clarifies his belief that all we know is what people do—some are "nice" and some "ain't nice but that's as far as any man got a right to say." Casy's new religion based on love and a belief in each man's soul, as well as an all-inclusive soul, the "Holy Spirit" of man, is derived from American ideas found primarily, critics explain, in Whitman and Emerson. Casy is a newly arrived transcendentalist who has paid some dues at least on the pragmatic level. For the time being, Tom remains a pragmatic ex-con less concerned with ethics than with finding his family and keeping the prison record to himself.[9]

Throughout the novel appear many figures involved with the Joads or in the activities of the time. By his own count, Muley Graves is no failure. He is not only a family man but a rebel who stays on, he insists, because he belongs there. Because roots are in the land, he will not leave. Tom and Jim realize that Muley's fight is hopeless. Another sharply etched figure is the used-car dealer, a fast talker and parasite who prospers from the troubles of others. The semi-driver who gives Tom a lift is far less harassed and threatened than most others in the novel. He will ride out the Depression trying to concentrate on memory courses and company rules. If the company survives, he will also. But he lacks Tom's courage and honesty.

As these comments on the introductory chapters suggest, *The Grapes of Wrath* can be read not only as fiction but as a social document of the time: a record of drought conditions, economic problems, the sharecropping life. Not separate from the fictional, this level or record is a vital aspect of it. The document clarifies the nature of family and small farm life and also of underlying concepts. One of the most important is the traditional agrarian idea of the simple rural life based on principles of natural rights. Those who live and work on the land, who pay for it with their blood, sweat, and toil, own the land.[10] Muley Graves believes this, and up to a point so do the Joads. This way of life is seriously threatened by nature and, more ominously, by another tradition, a largely modern one that has reappeared in recent years: the combination of big farms and financial establishments. A compassionate advocate of the first tradition and a bitter critic of the second, Steinbeck dramatizes their confrontation in chapter 5 as the owners, banks, and tractors push the tenants off the land. The bank or company is a monster that lives on profits, and those who do not produce profits are expendable. As the owners explain, everything is impersonal and mechanical. Nothing is anyone's fault.

Consequences of the clashes between these traditions and forces are dramatized by the Joads, who, deprived of their family home and temporarily residing at Uncle John's, also soon to be lost, gather around another symbol of the family condition. The Hudson Super Six, which is put together by Pa and Al, is not a marvel of ingenuity or construction, but can serve as both shelter and conveyance. The last family meeting on the land occurs around the Hudson. As it goes, so goes the family. Loaded down with thirteen people, boxes of clothing, kitchenware, tools, and also mattresses, chairs, a tent, and two barrels of salted-down fresh pork, the Hudson is a makeshift, dust-bowl version of the mobile home of later decades. It is also the covered wagon of the Depression migrants.

The westward journey of the Joads takes them some eighteen hundred miles through parts of seven states, "Texas and Oklahoma, Kansas and Arkansas, New Mexico, Arizona, California." The vast territory crossed in chapters 12–18 is described in Whitmanesque prose listing place names, state roads, and highways, as well as describing the national Highway 66, the main route westward, beginning for the Joads at Sallisaw: "the path of a people in flight, refugees from dust and shrinking land . . . shrinking ownership." The poetic commentaries of the land through which Highway 66 passes are effective because place names are often native to state or locale, and the continuous rhythms and idiomatic diction create a sense of expansiveness. The Joads and anonymous fami-

lies from the red and gray country of Oklahoma are joined
by thousands coming into Highway 66 from seemingly
hundreds of towns and roads:

270 up from McAlester. 81 from Wichita Falls south . . .
Hydro, Elk City, and Texola; and there's an end to Oklahoma. . . . And now the high mountains, Holbrook and Win-
slow and Flagstaff in . . . Arizona. Then the great plateau
rolling like a ground swell. . . . Then out of the broken
sun-rotted mountains of Arizona to the Colorado . . . and
that's the end of Arizona. There's California just over the
river . . .

Each middle chapter begins with a description of country the Joads on 66 are seeing for the first time. The vast
seemingly endless area suggests the scope of the problem.
Not only is it regional, it is national as well.

The migration of hundreds of thousands of people
westward was a major cultural phenomenon of the 1930s.
Steinbeck's portrayal of that phenomenon is another example of *The Grapes of Wrath* as a form of social document. Newspapers and magazines then provided a daily
and weekly coverage of a migration unique in a country
of migrations, which began in the 1700s with the westward
journeys into the Ohio Valley and regions south of the
Appalachians and include the gold rush in the 1850s and
the later Homestead migrations and settlements. In 1939,
*Fortune* carried an article, "I Wonder Where We Can
Go Now," describing the 1930s migrants, their backgrounds and experiences, and their reception in California.
The magazine editors explained that typical migrants
were not "habitual" ones but "removal" migrants who,
losing land or jobs, were forced into the life.[11] Drawing
upon his own sources and particularly on his years of
experience with migratory people and rural areas, Steinbeck brings that life back again in the pages of *The Grapes
of Wrath*.

In the middle chapters, the westward stream of im-
pecunious people is hardly welcomed by natives of the

various states. Hundreds of cars and trucks going by daily are reminders of economic dislocations, and, whether on Highway 66 or any other road, they bring little business. Steinbeck brilliantly describes reactions of anonymous small businessmen who, to profit on sales of car parts or food, cannot be lenient. They must manipulate prices and costs. Big businessmen as well resent strangers who symbolize economic troubles for them: high taxes, powerful labor unions, government interference.

Steinbeck's explanations of the conflicts are only partly convincing because at times the abstractions and documentaries tend to oversimplify, as in chapter 14: the haves are not that grasping and the have-nots are not that deserving. The intercalary chapters carry various warnings. The "great owners" must learn to distinguish between causes and "results": unions, taxes, or thousands of needy migrants are not causes but results; insufficient food and inadequate housing are causes. Big and small owners must recognize also that if the migrants ever organize their threat to the financial establishment will become immeasurably greater. The figurative grapes of wrath are ripening.

While anonymous families suggest the scope of economic and social conflicts, the Joads powerfully dramatize such conflicts. An essential part of the novel as social document, the Joads appear on a more fictional level as counterparts of the Old Testament Jews, engaged in their own archetypal search for a better way of life. They undergo many initiations. Ominously, one Joad dies near the beginning of the journey and another near the end. Neither grandparent can survive for long their separation from the land. During their journey the Joads are viewed, like the ancient Jews, with indifference, contempt, and hostility. There are also problems within the family. Preoccupied with her condition, discomforts of the ride, and daydreams of the future, Rose of Sharon is of little help to anyone in the Hudson. Husband Connie, who wanted to remain in Oklahoma, keeps to himself and says little. His plans to get a radio job somewhere anticipate his later disappearance. Uncle John appears frustrated, and the kids Ruthie and Winfield are often restless.

At times the family discovers that it cannot do everything alone. This realization is pressed upon them shortly after they meet the Wilsons and discover that Grandpa is dying. The Wilsons offer advice and material assistance. In this early scene of communal cooperation, the dying man is placed on the Wilson cot and covered with a blanket in their tent. After his death, the Joad men dig the grave and bury the Wilson blanket and Bible page with the body. Family identities are thereby merged. As everyone gathers around the grave, all listen to Jim Casy's Emersonian prayer. Afterwards Jim consoles Mrs. Wilson, who had earlier consoled Ma Joad. At this stage, however, the family can usually still act on its own. Ma faces down Tom and Jim, who want to split the family in two, tells the Jehovite woman to leave the tent, and gets angry at the deputy sheriff.

The family men make their own contributions, aided and abetted at times by Jim Casy. Although Pa Joad falters in disagreements with Ma, his common sense and steadiness compensate for John's worries and Connie's indifference. Tom and Al, in turn, compensate for the father's lack of firmness with their own determination to keep the Hudson and the Wilson Dodge patched up and going. The two vehicles, especially the Hudson, illustrate the sacrifices and skills of two brothers. Each controls his own bitterness, sense of inferiority, or sexual frustration in order to keep the families moving. Tom, who sometimes forgets that he is out on parole, repairs things when Al cannot. Al, who is trying to prove himself, learns from Tom that he already has proven himself. During the journey, Tom is primarily the empiricist, concerned with the here, now, it, or them. That may be a car to fix, "a little piece of iron and babbit" to repair, a place to stay, and, when he is irritated, people like the gas-station operator, a used-parts attendant, and a camp proprietor to tell off. When thinker Jim explains that there is a movement in the country, that something is happening that people do not understand, Tom tells him that he cannot think or worry about it. He will take one step at a time and climb fences when "I got fences to climb."

That general attitude, shared by most others in the family, must inevitably change. There are greater troubles ahead, as various minor characters appearing along Highway 66 seem to warn. These are usually two-dimensioned, allegorical figures buffeted by economic pressures. The gas-station owner, too frightened to sense what is happening, reminds the Joads of their own problems. The one-eyed man and ragged man are typical Steinbeck failures. The escapism of the first and the sad misfortunes of the second foreshadow later Joad losses and misfortunes. The ragged man explicitly warns the Joads, who do not heed the warning, and the camp proprietor represents a mentality that will mean trouble later. A small owner, he insists on payment before he will give an inch to anyone. While camping by the Colorado River, the Joads receive additional warnings from the relatively normal man and his son and also from both the Jehovite woman and officer—ominous stereotypes of bigotry and potential brutality. It is at the river also that the Joads hear for the first time the strange name of "Okie."

In the Great Central Valley—or some three hundred and fifty miles of it stretching from Needles near the Arizona border to Pixley—the westward migration ends for the Joads, as it did for hundreds of thousands in the 1930s.[12] As fiction and as social document, accounts in chapters 19–30 attest to past and present conditions in the Valley. Clearly the land is no Canaan, no "promised land," at least not for the Joads and likely not for their real-life counterparts. For many decades, the land has belonged to earlier occupants. Chapter 19 provides grim descriptions of Mexican ownership in the early 1800s, the arrival of Americans, or the "new barbarians," their gradual takeover, and the history of their prosperity and aggrandisement. Chapters 21 and 25 describe the later migrant "barbarians" of the 1930s and their con- flicts with the big owners who care nothing for the "Okies" or their needs. As owners and their operators control most of the best land, small owners are few.

The agrarian way of life—particularly for the mi- grants—has practically disappeared. The anonymous fam- ilies of chapter 1, reappearing in the third part, find little evidence of it; they encounter hardships greater than those in *In Dubious Battle* and *Of Mice and Men.* In *In Dubious Battle,* it is largely men alone who suffer. In *Grapes of Wrath,* entire families work for little pay or struggle along without it. They do not generally live in a well-kept camp, as in the strike novel, but in shelters of "gunny sacks" and subsist on diets of "biled nettles and fried dough." Their camps are often harassed or even burned out by angry Californians. Migrant problems do not seem to diminish but increase. The families in chapter 29, having survived droughts and all else, now encounter drenching rains, even less employment, and frightening rises of hostility and illness. The conflict between the two sides has grown desperate and violent.

The severity of the portrayal not only suggests the anger Steinbeck no doubt felt over conditions he had ob- served in California, but points to a naturalistic and alle- gorical emphasis on the hardships of the migrants, the inevitability of continued difficulties, and their inability to do anything significant about them. Such emphases appear earlier in the novel, but in this part, as several critics have indicated, the emphases are not in effect moderated by the presence of factors that could lighten the gloom a little, that would indicate the possibility of some kind of positive action by the Joads.[13]

This complex matter can be examined briefly first in terms of the Joads' experiences at the different stops or camps in California. While these stops reflect an oppressive reality, it is not without stabilizing and reassuring elements. The picture is less simplistic than it appears. The Hooverville camp provides no work and Connie and Casy leave, but Tom and Al respond well and Ma tells the family that they, "the people," will keep moving on. The Weedpatch episode, which represents one form of group or communal identity, necessitates a sacrifice of some family prerequisites. The Joads are equal to the occasion, however, and regain their self-respect though they find little work. Work and a better diet are available at the Hooper camp. The price of both is an outburst of violence that takes Jim's life, changes Tom's, and ironically strengthens the family resolve. The boxcar camp provides shelter, work, food, and helpful neighbors, but Tom must leave and Sharon loses her child. Tom's own determination strengthens the mother's, but further weakens the family. Pa Joad, John, and Al are unable to keep back the flood waters and to save the Hudson. Their spirit and determination are not defeated, however. In the black barn, the last and most temporary of shelters, Ma and Rose of Sharon combine strengths and do for the starving man what could not be done for the stillborn child.

Characters in this part, however—with one exception—do not regularly show the complexity or realism of figures in earlier chapters because of the writer's excessive reliance on allegorical or abstract elements. The one exception is Ma Joad, who, whether advising Rose of Sharon, keeping track of Ruthie or Winfield, thoughtfully coercing Pa Joad, or wondering about Tom, is generally credible. The strongest figure in the novel, she is a far stronger mother than Mrs. Wicks and Mrs. Munroe of *The Pastures of Heaven,* who live community-centered lives usually in imitation of their husbands. In her understanding of men and of the nitty-gritty aspects of life, Ma

resembles Rama Wayne of *To a God Unknown,* though
she lacks her sexuality and contempt for men. Both
women possess strong love for children, as does Mrs. Tiflin,
Jody's mother in *The Red Pony,* another sensible woman,
capable and warm. She is not, however, confronted with
great problems and burdens. Ma, who is, can cope with
most of them. She recognizes that in times of crisis and
loss of family members, others come first. The family
does not. Like Rama and Mrs. Tiflin, she is wise in the
ways of people and women, expressing belief in female
awareness of eternal life forces and in the importance of
courage and endurance.[14]

Although other characters do not lack tenacity and
sometimes purpose, the allegorical emphasis on their ideas
or stances noticeably dilutes the realism. Pa's sporadic
maturing in the last chapters is less indicative of failures
of nerve or of insight than of the pervasive theme that a
man who has lost his land may well lose his identity.
Tom Joad and Jim Casy loom far more importantly in
the closing chapters. Outside the Hooper camp, Jim appears as a new kind of strike leader not found in *In
Dubious Battle:* someone combining compassion for workers and children and ideas about cooperation and sacrifice.
In this last appearance, Jim symbolizes both Christian
views—his last words resemble those of Christ—and a
pragmatic transcendentalism explained months before to
Tom on the dusty Oklahoma road. Tom, his disciple, and
Ma Joad meet later in the cave. Tom speaks eloquently
of the future, of people all working "together for our
own thing—all farm our own lan'." He, too, stresses cooperation, for a person's soul is not his alone but is a
part of the whole. In his articulation of the Emersonian-
Whitmanesque idea preached by Jim, Tom is an advocate
of a new agrarianism. If he survives, he may later become
a leader in one of the large government camps.

However, the credibility of both scenes is diminished
somewhat by sketchy or abstract portrayal of place and

character. Both the scene outside the Hooper camp and the cave scene appear to be stages for the exposition of ideas as much as for their dramatization. The ideas are powerfully advanced, but the figures—especially outside Hooper—are vague. Jim is not a presence so much as a persuasive and familiar voice. He is not really shown. Ma Joad's presence and the confines of the cave make the later scene more concrete; and Tom is a familiar figure. Yet his praiseworthy ideas are more convincing in theory than in fact, because—since the Hooper violence especially —Tom's mulling over ideas and meanings, his attempts to work out a philosophy or general attitude have not been shown. In other words, Tom's rebirth in the cave, with its Freudian implications, is not adequately prepared for.[15]

The dreams and failures of the Joads, the conflicts between the haves and have-nots, the searches for land and a viable identity, culminate in the rain-soaked barn as an exhausted Rose of Sharon nurses a starving man. This remarkable scene has been praised for its portrayal of themes of cooperation and sacrifice and for its technical brilliance. The scene has been also criticized for failures in both respects. The chief failure appears to be one of motivation: although Rose of Sharon had riskily volunteered for cotton picking and faced the trials of birth bravely, she lacks the confidence and selflessness to act as shown in the barn. In allegorical terms the portrayal of Rose of Sharon may be convincing. In realistic terms it is not.

In thematic terms, the barn scene serves to illustrate and unify. The anonymous watchful women of chapter 1 have been replaced by a mother and daughter acting in a strange land to save a dying man. Rose of Sharon's action can be regarded as a form of communion, the giving of life. The Joads and the unidentified father and son are brought together in one family, a realization of Ma's earlier thoughts about the changes in families. Although the land and barn are privately owned, the relentless pressures of nature and society have compelled the have-nots to cooperate in order to survive. The meetings of families on Highway 66 have led to a new form of co-operation in which family identities and functions merge, and in which individuals sacrifice for the benefit of others. Rose of Sharon's sacrifice is comparable to Tom's going forth to lead and preach. Casy's gospel, the vision of Tom Joad, the strength and sacrifice of the women, and Steinbeck's essential humanity, all gain some realization in this final scene.

# 5

## Wartime Heroes and Communities

To escape the intrusive publicity and lionizing that accompanied the great success of *The Grapes of Wrath* and to continue explorations with Ed Ricketts of shoreline life and ecology, Steinbeck decided to take an extended trip south of California in the spring of 1940. During the previous year the two men had explored littoral life north of San Francisco and had decided on a bigger venture. Everything for it was carefully planned. They made inquiries of the U.S. State Department, obtained permission of the Mexican government, looked over various ships before deciding on one, and, no less important, found a good crew. The ship was the *Western Flyer*, a seventy-six-foot purse seiner, virtually new and in excellent condition, chartered from the owner and captain. Large enough for the captain, Ricketts, Steinbeck, an engineer, two sailors, and Carol Steinbeck, the *Western Flyer* was supplied with everything necessary to keep everyone occupied and healthy for a journey of over three thousand miles. Departing from Monterey harbor on 11 March 1940, they traveled south along the California and Mexican coasts and then north into the Gulf, stopping almost daily to collect specimens; they returned to Monterey on 20 April.[1]

The book about the expedition, *Sea of Cortez: A Leisurely Journal of Travel and Research* (1941), consists of two parts, the narrative account or log describing daily

activities of the journey and including opinions and speculations on sundry matters, and the "Annotated Phyletic
Catalogue" containing highly technical information on the
hundreds of specimens that they found in the Gulf. Until
recently it had always been thought that Steinbeck wrote
the log and Ricketts compiled the technical catalogue.
That assumption has recently been proven incorrect by
Richard Astro, who, after studying all relevant materials,
concluded that the log was actually a collaboration by
Steinbeck and Ricketts. Steinbeck had kept no journal
during the expedition, but Ricketts and the captain had
each compiled one. Relying largely upon the detailed
journal kept by Ricketts and to some extent on his own
recollections and talks with him, Steinbeck wrote the log
of the lengthy expedition. Astro makes clear that while
Steinbeck carefully planned and wrote the log, the im-
print of his friend's ideas and attitudes is evident throughout.[2] As the nature of the collaboration is intricate, to
simplify matters the narrator of the log will be referred
to as Steinbeck.

   *Sea of Cortez* is a remarkable work that combines
qualities of both fiction and nonfiction; in this respect it
can be compared to Thoreau's *Walden* and Melville's
*Moby-Dick*, other first-person narratives involving journeys, studies of bodies of water and their inhabitants, a
good deal of speculative energy, and a mixture of the
romantic, realistic, and skeptical. There are resemblances
between the roles and stances of the first-person narrators
and the structuring of materials in *Moby-Dick* and *Sea
of Cortez*. Fictional qualities in *Sea of Cortez* include the
narratives, which can present both imaginary and actual
experiences; a narrator who may be regarded as a poet,
scientist, and writer somewhat in the manner of Ishmael,
or, for that matter, in the manner of Steinbeck; and
scenes of dialogue and incident involving most of the
travelers. The narrator may be regarded at times as a
quester in the romantic sense of searching beyond the

material and scientific for overall or mythical meaning. The more markedly nonfictional elements of *Sea of Cortez* are description, exposition, and analysis which even in fiction can be essentially objective or factual and yet not obtrusive; and a narrator as lay biologist who provides generally objective expositions of a specimen, descriptions of a genus, and accounts of shore environment and habitat. Most chapters contain such materials.

The chief structural pattern of *Sea of Cortez* is that of the narrator's attempt to portray "the pattern of a reality controlled and shaped by the mind." Steinbeck explains the book's design as follows: "We have decided to let it form itself: its boundaries a boat and a sea; its duration a six weeks' charter time; its subject everything we could see and think and even imagine; its limits— our own without reservation." These essentially romantic comments remind us again of the authors and narrators of *Walden* and *Moby-Dick*, who regarded their nature experiences and the creative reshaping of them as largely organic. But in more literal terms, the narrator's ability to describe the concrete and pragmatic with consistent accuracy, to orient these and the more speculative elements within a day-by-day narrative pattern, and to combine all within a chronological discourse that is alternately factual, poetic, somber, humorous, analytic, and inclusive—these comprise the essentials of the unity in all three books.

Many aspects of *Sea of Cortez* may be profitably studied. Two will be considered here.

Communities in the book illustrate to some extent the biological ideas that helped shape Steinbeck's fiction of the 1930s and later. The ship community itself is not an example of group-men or commensal unity in a technical sense. The individuals get along well because they are professionals with common purposes and interests. They are handpicked and perform their functions efficiently. They do not, however, submerge their identities beneath a group identity. Steinbeck and Ricketts, as experts in littoral life, collect, examine, and classify hundreds of specimens, and they teach the others to locate and collect them. Tony Berry, the captain, and Tex, the engineer, are also highly skilled men who share a belief in the code of skill and experience. Tiny and Sparky, who are sailors and fishermen aboard ship, are competent and easygoing. Lacking the technical knowledge and interest that keep the others at times preoccupied, these two men also do much of the cooking and cleaning and gladly share in the beer drinking. Their attempts to catch fish or harpoon huge manta rays provide breaks in the narrative accounts. The six men work well together, seldom letting up during collecting hours; they form a good team. Carol Steinbeck and Ed Ricketts are not referred to by name, and Carol is referred to only indirectly and in passing. Ricketts's presence and attitudes are evident throughout.

A large if somewhat indeterminate community is formed by the many natives the men meet in the Gulf area. These include people in villages, visitors to the ship, officials who receive them on shore, and, at almost any stop, if a village is nearby, boys of all ages and sizes who come with specimens to trade or out of curiosity. In San Lucas there are also the young men who stand around the cantina waiting for the miracle of someone to buy them drinks. At Puerto Escondido the Americans meet the local teacher and others who take them sheep hunting in the nearby mountains.

Steinbeck does not treat the natives in a group-man sense, but his comments on them are not necessarily favorable. The expected contrasts between Americans and natives attest to the simplicity and peacefulness of native life. Village life in Loreto, for example, is free of the complications and distractions of technology and commerce in the United States. Yet Steinbeck concludes at one point that happiness and unhappiness seem to be about the same in both communities, and that native life is "just as full of nonsense as ours." There is frank recognition of weaknesses in both communities and restrained comment on strengths.

The most prominent community in *Sea of Cortez* is of course nature, the life and conditions along the Gulf shore, which are examined with the dedication and interest of Thoreau, who had much less to study at Walden pond and much more time in which to do so. As one might expect, the examinations by Steinbeck and Ricketts are far more scientific. They have aboard ship technical books on Gulf and Panamanian fauna, large and small-scale tide and coastal maps and charts, excellent collecting equipment, containers and preservatives of all kinds, microscopes, and the like. During their weeks in the Gulf and after many hours of collecting daily, they manage to collect some five hundred and fifty different specimens, about ten percent of which they later discover are new or unrecorded. In traveling from one stop to another, they see also many sharks, turtles, manta rays, and countless schools of fish. The littoral life itself is generally abundant. One or two species dominate a particular area, but usually life is a pitched battle with reproduction and survival the two key factors. The tide-pool metaphor for this book is the shoreline extending for hundreds of miles. As Steinbeck makes clear time and again, "All life is relational," and a key point in the Steinbeck-Ricketts approach is that men searching for specimens comprise part of that relationship.

A distinctive feature of the relational stance in *Sea of Cortez* is that it enables Steinbeck to comment on a variety of topics and ideas involving the ship, gulf water or something ashore. The topics include Charles Darwin, sea monsters, women at sea, fairy tales, symbols, scientific writing, native churches, and boat motors. All seem to fit in somehow and to reflect the writer's enthusiasm and curiosity. Both qualities are apparent in discussions or speculations of ideas, whether scientific or nonscientific.

The most vital and far-reaching idea is that of "is-thinking"—the lengthy discussion of which in chapter 14 is based on Ricketts's diary.[3] Regarded by Astro and Fontenrose, among others, as essential to an understanding of views in Steinbeck's fiction, these pages in *Sea of Cortez* elaborate on ideas advanced by Doc Burton in *In Dubious Battle* and found elsewhere in the fiction.[4] Drawing upon Ricketts's explanations of "three distinctive types of thinking," Steinbeck distinguishes between teleological and nonteleological thinking. The latter is not concerned with causes, validity, or moral values, but with processes and relationships, with things as they are and as they are related to other things. A sand crab must be examined in itself, in terms of its environment, and in relation to other animals in that environment. That environment in turn must be related to other environments, and so on. Man, a part of the environment or ecology, has a place in respect to all other individual animals and species. The purpose of nonteleological or "is-thinking" is to observe all such organisms and processes as objectively as possible with concern for the how or what, not the why, and for the overall picture.

As various commentators have explained, however, the concern with facts, processes, and the overall picture can lead to or involve somehow mystical views of relations and unity. The approach becomes romantic in the stress on feeling and on organic unity of all things.[5] In the *Log* we read:

Our own interest lay in relationships of animal to animal. If one observes in this relational sense, it seems apparent that species are only commas in a sentence, that each species is at once the point and the base of a pyramid, that all life is relational to the point where an Einsteinian relativity seems to emerge. And then not only the meaning but the feeling about species grows misty. One merges into another, groups melt into ecological groups until the time when what we know as life meets and enters what we think of as non-life. . . . And it is a strange thing that most of the feeling we call religious, most of the mystical out-crying . . . is really the understanding and the attempt to say that man is related to the whole thing, related inextric-ably to all reality, known and unknowable.

Among other things, this passage suggests the broad philosophic base from which Steinbeck writes in *Sea of Cortez*. He is as prepared to make moral judgments as to make relatively objective or scientific comments. The re-lational view expressed here and the fairly episodic na-ture of the work account in large part for its flexibility and range. Thus, we find in Steinbeck's examination of beginnings an interesting account of man's prehuman in-stinctual qualities, some attributable to the Precambrian influences of tides and moon phases upon all living things. He discusses other influences, among them the racial un-conscious and the rich harvest of symbols that "seem to have been planted in the soft rich soil of our pre-human-ity."

The writer's hatred of war is obvious. Regarded as inherently warlike, man possesses a trait "which causes the individual to turn on and destroy his own kind, not only his own kind, but the words of his own kind." Hope, which Steinbeck regards as "another species diagnostic trait," cannot be of much help. If man is to eradicate or change war, a mutation must occur not in man but in outside things—"property, houses, money, concepts of power . . . cities . . . factories . . . business." One on-going mutation condemned by the writer is the industrial revolution, the consequences of which are fundamental. The tendency toward collectivism—the mechanized army and assembly line are examples—would represent a sim-ilar kind of mutation, and, as Steinbeck sees it, a fore-boding one, for "it is a rule in paleontology that orna-mentation and complication precede extinction."

Other speculative discussions—of social organization, scientific hypotheses, happiness, peaceful native villages—

appear more balanced and are no less interesting. Ranging in tone and view from the pragmatic and scientific to the subjective and romantic, *Sea of Cortez* is one of Steinbeck's richest works.

The Japanese attack on Pearl Harbor occurred in December 1941, the month *Sea of Cortez* appeared. Too old at thirty-nine for military service, Steinbeck was nevertheless involved. He wrote *Bombs Away* (1942), a very successful Air Corps training book, covered the war as a correspondent in Europe in 1943, and also wrote two novels, one of them about the war.

The idea for *The Moon Is Down* (1942) grew out of conversations in 1941 with William J. Donovan, head of the wartime OSS, on ways of assisting resistance groups in occupied countries. As Norway had been invaded by German military forces in April 1940, underground resistance was a fact of life in Norway during the war years. While neither enemy nor resisting country is identified in the novel, general resemblances to the Norwegian occupation are apparent. The action centers on a small coastal town quickly subdued by enemy forces. The commanding officer, an intelligent realist, and his fellow officers issue orders from the top floor of the mayor's house. Compelled to mine coal for the invading country, the townspeople try to resist. An officer is killed; the accused is tried and executed; in revenge, the man's wife kills another officer. Resistance continues. The mayor and the doctor are arrested, and the mayor is condemned to death. The novel ends with the mayor's speech on democratic principles.

Wartime reactions to *The Moon Is Down* included both angry protests against allegedly complacent treatments of the Nazi occupation and praise from Norwegian officials for truthful portrayals of the resistance.[6] The literary merits were generally ignored as readers formed judgments on the basis of national allegiances and personal experiences.

Unfortunately, the literary opinion about the novel from the 1940s up to the present has been unfavorable. Steinbeck's ability to create something new or different seemed each time to have failed in 1942. As his second experiment with the novel-play form, *The Moon Is Down* is seriously flawed by the writer's lack of firsthand knowledge. No stranger to violence or group conflict, Steinbeck was nonetheless thousands of miles away from war and the Norwegian occupation. The lack of knowledge and reliance upon the novel-play form very likely account for the generally thin realism. The coastal town itself is either vaguely or else impressionistically portrayed. The descriptions, combining parable and drama, create a sense of unrealness: "The dark buildings of the little town wore bells and hats and eyebrows of white and there were trenches through the snow to the doorways." Action has expectedly a drawing-room quality: there is little impression of wartime realism because of the stress upon scenes and dialogue set mainly in the mayor's home. Active resistance and conflicts, in effect, occur offstage. Only indirectly do we learn of the invasion, Alex's execution, and of the seduction-murder encounter of Molly and Lieutenant Tender, not to mention the many dynamitings, parachutings, and other machinations of the resistance.

Opposing communities in *The Moon Is Down* understandably lack the verisimilitude of the haves and have-nots in *In Dubious Battle*. The townspeople exist not by hundreds but by the handfuls. The selected persons entering from offstage are typical and do give a sense, if not a strong one, of the values and practices of the traditionally free community. The townspeople illustrate some qualities of the group-man concept in the actions of the butler and maid and perhaps in the cohesion and goals of the community after the execution. Characters such as Mr. Orden, Dr. Winters, and the paradoxical Corell, with his war-machine mentality, keep their individualities. The invading community represents at times the military version of a group-man organism. Each man has his military duty and role and fulfills it, and Loft and Prackle talk and act like militarists. Both Hunter and Lanser recognize the need for conformity and obedience, and Colonel Lanser in particular is familiar with the workings of the military organism. Yet, as can now be noted, the impression of soldiers and officers as group-men is only occasional.

Portrayals of some military figures and townspeople occasionally revitalize the novel. Steinbeck sensibly did not fall back on stereotyped characterizations of either subhuman or extraordinary officers and men. Many are credible as individuals. Major Hunter is convincing as an engineer more interested in the drawing board and plans than in people and issues, and the self-pitying Lieutenant Tender is individualized by his sincere but naive attempts to seduce Molly Morden and to escape the war. Captain Loft is honest enough to admit that he is an opportunist. Except for Annie and Joseph, who appear overly predictable as scheming likeable servants, the townspeople are credible. Molly Morden is not without sensitivity as she quietly plans to avenge her husband's murder, and Dr. Winter, a philosophic spokesman in the novel, is believably steady and knowledgeable.

As wartime heroes and individualists, Mayor Orden and Colonel Lanser add substance and realistic purpose to *The Moon Is Down*. Prosaic and bumbling, Orden has the views of someone raised in a democratic community. Aware of his limitations and the expectations of the townspeople, he lacks pretensions and vanity. He is a sturdy realist upholding community ideals. The more complex Lanser is both an "is-thinker" concerned with processes, and a teleologist sensitive to moral and social values. While caring little for power or leadership as such, Lan-

ser follows orders, knowing that the town will disregard
them and eventually regain its freedom. Both Orden and
Lanser are three-dimensional figures.

After returning to the United States in 1943, Steinbeck wrote another book about the war, but weary of
war talk and activity he decided not to publish it. Knowing that civilians in general and GI's in particular wanted
to read something peaceful and funny, Steinbeck, mulling over pleasant experiences in the 1930s, decided on a
second novel about Monterey, California, or rather about
one area of that celebrated town.

Written in only six weeks and seemingly a labor of
love, *Cannery Row* (1945) became one of Steinbeck's
most popular works. Like *Sea of Cortez* published a few
years earlier, the novel was profoundly influenced by the
mind, character and life of Ed Ricketts. *Cannery Row*
begins with the inscription: "For Ed Ricketts, who knows
why or should." In the novel, Ricketts becomes Doc,
biologist and the owner of Western Biological Laboratory,
who lives in the Row, a bohemian section near the fish
canneries in Monterey. Doc, his lab, and his way of life
comprise the nucleus of the small community. Across the
street from the lab is Lee Chong's grocery, and in the
vacant lot next to the grocery live Mack and the boys.
Also sharing the lot are Dora's Bear Flag Restaurant, a
respectable whorehouse, and a married couple who live
nearby in a huge deserted cannery boiler.

As celebrated in Steinbeck's fiction as the Flat of
*Tortilla Flat* (1935), the Row is a low-rent area, relaxed,
unpretentious, but hardly dormant. Something is always
happening. The action begins with scenes of Lee Chong
and his grocery, moves a short distance to Dora's Bear
Flag Restaurant, then to Doc's lab, and to Mack and the
boys in the Palace Flophouse. Early in the novel the
reader learns about the suicides of Horace Abbeville and
the bouncer William, about the strange old Chinaman,

about Doc's collecting in the Tide Pool, and about Mr. and
Mrs. Mallory. In the middle chapters the focus is often
outside the Row as Doc collects octopi and Mack and the
boys capture hundreds of frogs. Upon their return Mack
and the boys arrange a big party for Doc, which gets out
of hand. When Doc returns, he is greatly distressed by the
results. The last chapters center on community efforts to
honor Doc with a big, peaceful party. It is a huge success.
Afterwards, Doc feels relaxed and contemplative.

Such characters and activities clearly link *Cannery
Row* and *Tortilla Flat*. Both novels are imaginative,
loosely unified, and at times brilliantly written.

The casual life-style and hedonic qualities also place
*Cannery Row* in the broad tradition of the western fiction
of Bret Harte and Jack London, who sometimes wrote of
individualistic, freewheeling ways of life. Although Harte's
gamblers, miners, and prostitutes played and worked under pressures the Row characters are generally free of,
nonetheless their camaraderie, independence, and indul-
gence recall the life depicted in *Cannery Row*. Jack London had a predilection for adventurers of a type that are
scarce in the Row, but drifters and bums are common in
both the Row and some fictions by London.

Like *Sea of Cortez, Cannery Row* is linked as well
to American romantic literature of the midnineteenth century. The inhabitants of the Row are romantics in their
casual defiance of traditional society. Mack, his boys, and
others live a relatively independent existence, illustrating
Emerson's dictum of doing your own thing. Others appear
less hedonic than dreamy and mysterious, thereby con-
tributing to the romantic aura. Doc may or may not be
considered a Thoreauvian character, but as a scientist he
finds in the tide pools evidence for nature's laws and for
the belief, also expressed in the *Sea of Cortez*, that all
living things are related.[7] The tide pool image, figuratively a part of the community, bears resemblances to
Thoreau's pond and possibly to Melville's ocean. These

and other romantic elements tend to be ironic, for not many things in the novel are truly heroic or exceptional.

The novel's unity can be puzzling, for on the first reading the thirty-two chapters and introduction may appear to be no more than a string of loosely related episodes or stories. The eleven or twelve interchapters and their places in the development may be especially perplexing. In its episodic nature, *Cannery Row* resembles *The Pastures of Heaven* and *Tortilla Flat*. The novel differs from the latter in being less dependent upon myth and more dependent on place, and from the former in being fundamentally more unified. *Cannery Row* is in fact carefully structured by means of thematic contrasts and at times an organic development.

The introductory chapters 1–8 illustrate both points. The poetic beginning sets up the thematic contrasts of "a poem, a stink, a grating noise, a quality of life . . . [of] the gathered and scattered . . . laboratories and flophouses." Depending upon the peephole, inhabitants of the Row may be regarded as "whores, pimps, gamblers, and sons of bitches" and also as "Saints and angels and martyrs and holy men." Whether ironic or straightforward, contrasts of the routine and remarkable, of the seedy and beautiful, are found throughout. In the early chapters they appear in accounts of inhabitants who either die pathetically or live imaginatively, and they are embedded in descriptions of the buildings and of their ties to the inhabitants.

Lee Chong's grocery appears ordinary except to those who need whiskey, pork chops, lettuce, firecrackers, beer, tennis shoes, or almost anything else. The grocery, described as "very remarkable," is packed to the rafters with everything haphazardly in place. Chong himself is remarkable. The decrepit Abbeville building, until recently a dirty storage place for fishmeal, is converted by Mack and the boys into a first-rate flophouse, a marvelous mishmash of odds and ends, none of them purchased:

There were old carpets on the floor, chairs with and without seats. . . . A wicker chaise longue painted bright red . . . tables, a grandfather clock without dial face or works. The walls were whitewashed which made it almost light and airy. Pictures began to appear—mostly calendars showing improbable luscious blondes holding bottles of Coca-Cola. Henri had contributed two pieces from his chicken-feather period. A bundle of giltded cattails stood in one corner and a sheaf of peacock feathers was nailed to the wall beside the grandfather clock.

Dora's Bear Flag Restaurant comes under scrutiny, illustrating a variety of effects, but mostly the hedonic and sensual, controlled and purified as much as they can be. Doc's Western Biological Laboratory has its realistic and fabulous components under one roof, with shelves and tables of marine specimens and scientific equipment and also many books, paintings, and records. As packed as Chong's grocery, Doc's building is described inside and out, upstairs and down, as befits a place of great events, solitary and communal. Interchapters 2 and 4 are thematically related to descriptions of the Row and buildings, for they clarify the actual, intricate reality of the community and touch upon such themes as life and death, dream and fear.

The middle chapters begin with the agreement reached by Doc and Mack in chapter 9 and end with Doc's rightful outburst against the repentant sinner in chapter 21. In between, the lonely scientist goes on his quest for octopi, indulging en route in hamburgers and beer milk shakes, before he discovers along the beach not only octopi but also a beautiful dead woman. Mack and the boys, who are both sons of bitches and saints, steal and charm their way along, capturing frogs and sacrificing and indulging in a humorous pattern of contrasts.

The interchapters of the middle section also illustrate

something of the ordinary and exceptional, the ridiculous and the sublime. Frankie, who loves Doc more than most, can do little for him, and little can be done for Frankie, who is deserving himself. The rather gruesome incident involving Josh Billings's remains illustrates the attempts of the respectable to maintain the respectable. The happy soldiers and girls in chapter 14 are oblivious to matters of respectability. They couldn't care less about property and status. However, the social castoffs of the Row are capable of genuine community efforts, as shown in their fight against flu. These interchapters, showing thematic bases of the novel, contribute to the basic narrative thrust which ends with the robustious party and Doc's outburst.

Preparations for Doc's second party provide the dominant unifying pattern in chapters 22–32. Moods of the Row are sometimes gloomy or confused, and not all contributions to the party are unselfish. The prevailing tone, however, is positive and enthusiastic. It is clearly present during the party and especially during the brawl ending the party. This is not a common brawl, but a joyous celebration—with clubs, fists, bottles, and other manageable objects—of physical combat, a mock-heroic battle on Skid Row. The brawl solidifies the deep feelings that led to the party, and casts out any remaining loneliness and selfishness.

Interchapters 22, 24, 26, and 31 illustrate various thematic contrasts, and incidents in a few are directly related to the party. While most descriptions of Row activities are balanced between humor and irony, occasionally the writer's facility or his compassion make them sentimental. The account in chapter 25 of the spread of "a kind of gladness" through not only the Row but down along the shore and into the hearts of sea lions quickly becomes silly. Fortunately, few such excesses appear in *Cannery Row*.

While life in the Row community is hardly ideal, the

tension and divisiveness of earlier works are absent. The
Wayne families in *To a God Unknown* eventually separate; many leave the valley community in *The Pastures
of Heaven*. Danny and his boys do not stay together, and
the groups in *In Dubious Battle* and *Of Mice and Men* are
fragmented by economics and by human frailties. Even
when government camps in *The Grapes of Wrath* prove
adequate, most migrants move on because of outside pressures.

For many living on the Row, life is about as good as
it will ever be. It provides freedom. A man can sleep in
a boiler in the vacant lot, run up a grocery bill at Lee
Chong's, pay two dollars for a visit to Dora's, work a
little for Doc or in a nearby cannery. Or he can do
nothing. There is also tolerance. Various marginal people
live on the Row. Henri, the painter who is not a painter,
gets along well with Doc, who, showing tolerance for all,
gets along well with Albert, the bouncer, who, unlike his
predecessor, is on good terms with Mack and the boys.
Because most on the Row share in the poverty, hard luck,
or laziness, there is a strong sense of community. One
helps another because no one outside the community will.
And certainly the Row has more than its share of love.

Steinbeck's reply to Malcolm Cowley that *Cannery
Row* was indeed a "poisoned cream puff" attests to the
other side of the coin.[8] That other side is satire directed
at most aspects of life in *Cannery Row*. There is obvious
ridicule in references to middle-class and upper-class men
who slip unseen into Dora's place, to owners and admin-
istrators of canneries who drive sheltered in big cars to
and from their offices in the Row, and to police and city
officials who require big donations from Dora if she is to
stay in business. Middle-class respectabilities such as am-
bition, perseverance, industry, and dependability receive
their comeuppance because Mack, Eddie, Albert, and the
Mallorys put little faith in standards of the arrived or the

almost-arrived. Yet the Row figures do not escape re-
proach because they are not above displays of selfishness,
dishonesty, and immaturity. Mack's rejection of William,
the bouncer and pimp, leads to the man's suicide, and his
actions in the first party are stupid and destructive. But
generally Mack and the others appear to be more likeable
human beings than many middle-class characters in the
fiction.

Part of the satire and irony in *Cannery Row* lies in
the fact that principal figures combine bohemian and
middle-class qualities. Lee Chong and Dora Flood are
unique because they combine financial respectability and
compassion. Unlike their middle-class counterparts elsewhere in Monterey, Chong and Dora place financial values below human values. Through long-time loans to most
everyone in the Row, Lee has lost considerable sums of
money. He has also been charitable in other respects. After the suicide of Horace Abbeville, who had jokingly
admitted that he lacked credit for even a pack of gum
for his kids, Chong sees to it that no child in the Row
ever goes without a stick of spearmint chewing gum. A
man of natural dignity and integrity, Chong serves as an
example to others in the community.

What Dora Flood sells cannot be purchased on credit.
Her price for amenities, however, is reasonable and the
same for everyone. She runs a "decent, clean, honest, old-
fashioned sporting house," and she allows no one in her
establishment to raise prices. Dora and her establishment
are acceptable to the middle-class community because she
contributes valuable services and pays sizeable dues. At
times, however, the orange-haired madame, like the proprietor of Susy's in *Of Mice and Men,* or Faye and Jenny,
two erstwhile madams in *East of Eden,* becomes the sen-
timentalized whore with the good heart.

Ranking in Steinbeck's fiction with Ma and Tom
Joad, Jim Casy, and Jody Tiflin, and possessing salient

qualities of Doc Burton (*In Dubious Battle*) and Juan
Chicoy (*The Wayward Bus*), Doc is the central figure in
*Cannery Row*. Humanity and compassion are his fundamental qualities. Doc is always willing to help a needy
person, whether with a loan, food, or helpful advice.
He advises Dora's girls, and after the disastrous first
party he nevertheless speaks highly of Mack. If his love
affairs and sexual conquests are self-indulgent, they show
as well a healthy dependence upon others.

Doc's greatest strength lies in the ability to reconcile
extremes, to accept life's contradictions and ironies. "His
mind had no horizon—and his sympathy had no warp."
He is equal to most occasions and demands. When he
falters, he feels no bitterness. His loneliness reflects his
commitments to ideals and his search for the balanced
life. His great commitment to science gives life meaning
and direction. That interest and training account in part
for the tolerant acceptance of society's outcasts, failures,
and eccentrics. Doc does not "blame" Mack, and he is not
interested in the "causes" of Frankie's trouble. He wishes
to understand, and accepts the two as they are in the
scheme of things, thus reflecting ideas in the earlier *Sea of
Cortez*.

Doc's scientific interests are balanced by a deep love
and understanding of painting, music, and poetry. These
prove as necessary and as fulfilling as science. On the
walls of the library in Doc's place are

bookcases to the ceiling . . . books of all kinds, dictionaries,
encyclopedias, poetry, plays. A great phonograph stands
against the wall with hundreds of records lined up beside
it. . . . And on the walls and to the bookcases are pinned
reproductions of Daumier, and Graham, Titian, and Leonardo
and Picasso, Dali and George Grosz.

To escape the demands of science or the wearying indul-
gences of the Row, he sometimes listens to church music,
Gregorian chants, and to records of Monteverdi, Bee-

thoven, and Bach. These create a sense of peace and completeness. Translations of Sanskrit and Chinese poetry also contribute to the man's peace of mind and to his reverence for life and death. All are essential to Doc's unique and humane way of life.

# 6

# Postwar Allegory, Realism, and Romance

The war years, widely separated assignments, moves from one home to another, a new marriage, and a permanent residence in the East did not greatly change the shape and purpose of Steinbeck's fiction. The four novels appearing between 1947 and 1952 show the continued importance of western materials and a preoccupation with two familiar staples of his fiction, allegory and realism. Steinbeck's interest in allegory had appeared first in his boyhood love of *Morte d'Arthur,* a little later in characters and actions of a Stanford story, "The Gifts of Iban," and then in *Cup of Gold* (1929) and *To a God Unknown* (1933). Characters and actions representing ideas or attitudes, archetypal patterns, and a strong ethical focus— all qualities of allegory, and particularly of parable—appeared most noticeably in *Tortilla Flat* (1935).

Although such qualities are less vital in the realistic Depression novels, portrayals of Joy and Jim and of the strike confrontations in *In Dubious Battle* (1936) include an allegorical level stressing ideas or qualities. That emphasis appears also in the two-dimensional figures and specialized situations and patterns of *The Grapes of Wrath* (1939). *Cannery Row* (1945) may be regarded as primarily a parable, for, as Lawrence W. Jones explains, the novel includes, along with the usual features, "the shimmering designed world of the not-real" and a concern for moral issues, although it lacks the universalized dialogue and the controlling archetypal pattern of a complete parable.[1]

Important though allegory and parable are in the postwar fiction, they are no more so than another long-standing Steinbeckian predilection, the realistic, which goes back almost as far as his interest in allegory, appearing, for example, in "The Chrysanthemums" and "Flight" in the 1930s and also in the Depression novels. In fact, as we shall see, novels of the late 1940s and early 1950s reveal a weakening of the allegorical emphasis and a strengthening of Steinbeck's disposition toward both realism and the romantic, a blending of which is evident also in his earlier works, including *The Grapes of Wrath*.

An unsuccessful work can sometimes be more illustrative of a major writer's approach, particularly its weaknesses, than a skillfully constructed and well-written novel. This is true at least of *Burning Bright*, which will be discussed here because it demonstrates a failure of allegorical practices. Perhaps Steinbeck's least convincing effort, *Burning Bright*, which appeared in 1950 as both a novel and as a Broadway play, failed in each instance because Steinbeck's real interest was not in the imaginative possibilities of the materials but in contemporary ideas and character types. The settings of circus, farm, and ship appear significant, but they tell little about the theme of sterility and about the frustrated characters except to indicate their universality. The action centering around the husband Joe Saul, Mordeen, the wife, and her impregnation by Victor is at times thin and obvious. Joe Saul and Mordeen take part in realistic scenes, but the others do not. Friend Ed says the right things at the right times in a way that becomes unbelievable, and Victor's changes from brash assertiveness to troubled maturity lie on the surface. Remarks about sterility and love soon become simplistic. The potentially interesting combination of allegory and realism, of types and grim facts, remains awkward and unconvincing.

Such weaknesses do not appear in an earlier and far superior allegory, *The Pearl,* the idea for which occurred to Steinbeck during the sea expedition aboard the *Western Flyer* in 1940. *Sea of Cortez* (1941) had already referred to the story of a young Mexican and a great pearl, which appeared as "The Pearl of the World" in the *Woman's Home Companion,* December 1945, and as a novel in 1947.[2]

*The Pearl* is a parable, a modern morality fiction about one man's search for security, wealth, and freedom. The fairly involved action centers on Kino, a fisherman, his wife, Juana, and his infant son, Coyotito, who live in a small village on a beach in Mexico. One morning the son is stung by a scorpion. In an effort to obtain money for medical treatment, Kino finds a great pearl. The doctor in town treats the son, but he and others have evil designs on the pearl. During attempts to steal it, Kino is attacked. Warned by his brother and wife to get rid of the pearl, Kino keeps it because of his plans for the future. Fleeing the village, the family is attacked by three men. In the fight the men and the infant son are killed. After the anguished parents return to the village, Kino throws the great pearl back into the sea.

The principal allegorical elements are readily perceptible. Kino, Juana, and Coyotito are clearly good and innocent, and the mother and son remain so. The child itself is a symbolic pearl. The village illustrates the innocent life, while the much larger town represents a source of evil to the family. The prospective buyers of the pearl from the town are greedy, and the doctor is designing and cruel. The journey away from the village represents a venture into the unknown, danger, and evil. Various other situations and characters in *The Pearl* also have meanings about which most readers would likely agree.

Yet, the quotation preceding chapter 1—"If this story is a parable, perhaps everyone takes his own meaning from it and reads his own life into it"—correctly sug-

gests that actions in *The Pearl* possess a depth and richness of meaning absent in *Burning Bright*. The cruel
doctor's treatment may indeed benefit the son. Kino can
sensibly exchange the pearl for modest benefits, but, in attempting to gain the future, he disregards his brother,
kills his enemies, and beats his wife. A good man can be
led astray by an excessive concern for the material things
of life. Kino's actions lead finally to the death of Coyotito
—the greatest loss of all.

In this finely crafted work, the unreal mood of a
parable is beautifully sustained. *The Pearl* begins on a
peaceful early morning as the parents awaken and quietly
begin the day. Kino's people had once been makers of
songs. In the early hours, before the scorpion strikes, Kino
hears a song that, if he could speak of it, he would call
"The Song of the Family":

Outside the door he squatted down and gathered the blanket
ends about his knees. . . . Behind him Juana's fire leaped
into flame and threw spears of light through the chinks of
the brush-house wall and threw a wavering square of light
out the door. . . . The Song of the Family came now from
behind Kino. And the rhythm of the family song was the
grinding stone where Juana worked the corn for the morning
cakes.

The possession of the Pearl of the World creates a special music in Kino's mind. After the pearl has been returned to the sea, "the music of the pearl drifted to a
whisper and disappeared." Sea and animal imagery also
serve to relate the various activities of the family.
Throughout the parable, contrasts of place, individuals,
and communities, and the repetitions of action—leaving
and returning to the village, for example—illustrate ethical themes, all of which are expressed through a sensitive
prose.

Steinbeck's 1940 expedition with Ed Ricketts led
not only to *Sea of Cortez* and *The Pearl*, but also to *The*

*Wayward Bus* (1947), originally set in Mexico and intended to be "something like the *Don Quixote* of Mexico." Steinbeck, who enjoyed writing the novel, explained in a letter to his editor: "From the funny little story it is growing to the most ambitious thing I have ever attempted." [3] Prepublication sales of almost one million copies seemed to bear out the writer's high hopes for the work. Good sales continued into the early 1950s as readers found the characters and their plight absorbing. However, many discerning readers, then and later, have tended to be critical of the novel, citing as weaknesses static characterizations, slowly moving action, and awkward allegory. [4]

There is, however, the likelihood that *The Wayward Bus*, like *East of Eden*, has received more critical attention for its alleged weaknesses than for its actual strengths. The allegorical materials are in fact well managed. The allegory is introduced by a quotation from the first six lines of *Everyman*, a late-fifteenth-century morality play about a person who journeys to Death but can find no one to accompany him except Good Deeds. The quoted lines begin: "I pray you all gyve audyence, And here this mater with reverence, By fygure a morall playe; The somonynge of Everyman called it is." Most characters in *The Wayward Bus* exhibit allegorical qualities, and several may be regarded as representatives of modern *Everyman* figures: Camille Oaks as Beauty, Pimples as Five Wits, Van Brunt as Death, and Juan Chicoy possibly as Christ. [5] Good-natured Ernest Horton may be a modern-day Fellowship. Their journey is to some extent allegorical, for it includes several obstacles that convey a sense of universality, and it ends at night as the bus, a symbol either of mankind or of America, moves toward the small town or Death. Various minor points lend themselves to a parable-like treatment: the initials of Juan Chicoy; the religious words on the bus bumper (the

barely readable inscription "el Gran Poder de Jesus"—
the great power of Jesus); the small metal Virgin of
Guadalupe on the bus dashboard; and the religious signs
along the muddy road—"Repent, for the Kingdom of
Heaven is at hand."

The novel's chief strengths do not lie in allegory,
however, but in realism. Among the long works, only *The
Red Pony* is more pervasively realistic in portrayals of
things as they impress the senses. The trials and tribula-
tions of bus travel in postwar California are recorded with
care and accuracy. The allegorical materials and the satiric elements lie within and are subordinated to the actual. For the most part the integration of these is convincing.

Early descriptions in *The Wayward Bus* illustrate the
writer's preoccupation with the facts and things of everyday existence. After accounts in chapter 1 of the bus stop
at Rebel Corners, descriptions are given of the small
lunchroom there, the three tables, long counter, the silver
coffee urn, and the contents of shelves:

On the first shelf behind the counter were sweet rolls, snails,
doughnuts; on the second, canned soups, oranges, and
bananas; on the third, individual boxes of cornflakes, rice-
flakes, grapenuts, and other tortured cereals. There was a
grill at one end behind the counter and a sink beside it,
beer and soda spouts beside that, ice cream units beside
those, and on the counter itself, between the units of paper
napkin containers, juke-box coin slots, salt, pepper, and
ketchup, the cakes were displayed under large plastic covers.

Almost expectedly, there are descriptions also of flies
buzzing around the counter, of the screen door that lets
them in, of beds and dressers in the living quarters beyond and, outside, of the tall, graceful white oaks that
shelter the Corners and, close to the lunchroom, of the
blacksmith shop converted into a garage. Inside the garage stands the wayward bus under repair:

It was an old bus, a four-cyclinder, low-compression engine
with a special patented extra gear shift which gave it five
speeds ahead instead of three, two below the average ratio,
and two speeds in reverse. The ballooning sides of the bus,
heavy and shining with aluminum paint, showed nevertheless the bumps and bends, the wracks and scratches, of a
long and violent career.

Knowledgeable about the basics of motor vehicles, Steinbeck proceeds to elaborate on many features of the bus.

Leaving Rebel Corners, the group votes not to try
the bridge at Breed's, and Juan drives the bus along the
pitted, winding road toward San Ysidro. The history of
the road, the ditches full of weeds and wild flowers, the
redwood post fences and barbed wire, are described in
detail as the bus moves along. One implication is that
everyone aboard is influenced not only by others but
by the condition of the bus, the road, and the surround-
ings. Flood waters raging against the bridge at Breed's
appear less indicative of allegorical qualities than repre-
sentative of very real threats and obstacles along the way.
The old road upon which everyone is later stranded is
part of the here-and-now reality threatening to halt the
forward progress of mankind or a small group toward
Death or a small California city. Covering only a small
segment of the central California territory described in
*The Grapes of Wrath,* Rebel Corners and vicinity are presented with care and precision.

Bus passengers and inhabitants of Rebel Corners
alike—comprising a cross section of middle-class, midcen-
tury Americans—possess allegorical qualities, but these
are skillfully blended with the weightier realistic materials. If Juan Chicoy's initials and respect for the metal
Virgin of Guadalupe suggest that he may serve as a moral
guide in the movel, the dominant descriptions of him—
face, hands, and general appearance—convey no impression of extraordinary or allegorical strength and leader-

ship. They suggest rather that he is an experienced and capable man whose judgment can be trusted. In some respects he is the man Tom Joad might have become if things had turned out differently. Juan's courage and honesty set him apart. His acceptance of himself and tolerance of others reflect a fundamental confidence.

The realistic shaping of characters in the novel includes satirical as well as allegorical elements: most characters possess limitations or predilections that indicate Steinbeck's criticisms of postwar values. The salesman, Ernest Horton, toughened by infantry combat, is generally realistic, tolerant of others, and does not lack courage. Yet Horton is clearly out for the buck, bends a few principles in determined pursuit of it, and is fascinated by the gross gadgetry and deceptions he sells for the Little Wonder Company. But the satire is mild. Treatment of the relatively sophisticated Mr. Pritchard, however, is caustic. Described as "a businessman, president of a medium-sized corporation," and representing business values and success, Pritchard appears composed, commanding, and resolute. In fact, he is none of these. To enhance his self-image and ensure his confidence and success, Pritchard depends upon yes men in his company and an artificial marriage at home. When deprived of these supports, he founders. Within a few hours, he proves devious with Camille and Horton and brutal with his wife. Pritchard, in critic Peter Lisca's groupings, is one of the "damned." [6]

A typical teenager, Pimples, or Kit Carson, comes off relatively well. He works hard, assists Juan capably, and is courteous toward the carping Alice. But in his sexual fantasies and plans for a future in electronics, he is at times swayed as much by trends and obsessions of the day as is Norma. The least palpably realistic of these figures, the disagreeable Van Brunt symbolizes death; his strokes, rages, and warnings cast him also as a modern

prophet of doom. Yet in speech and manner, he is simply
a cross, misanthropic old man.

Although women characters are no less numerous and
prominent in *The Wayward Bus* than in *The Long Valley*
and *The Grapes of Wrath,* realistic portrayals predomi-
nate. Good-hearted whores, obsessed figures, with one exception, and strong mothers do not appear at Rebel Corners. Single women do appear and usually without the
familiar tags of promiscuity and frustration. Both Camille
Oaks and Mildred Pritchard, for example, are stable and
self-respecting. Camille manages to keep her sense of
values in a highly competitive, sex-centered society. Basi-
cally honest with herself and others, Camille regards her
job as a stripper as no more than an economic necessity.
She does not flaunt her sexuality, and in fact is mystified
by it. Mildred Pritchard, breaking away from family influences, may well become another postwar liberated
woman. She enjoys sex, feels no guilt about her affairs,
and realistically admits that the affair with Juan is over.
She recognizes her own flaws, and does not minimize
those of her parents.

Norma, a waitress with dreams and sensibilities, lacks
common sense. She worships Clark Gable, seriously daydreams about an independent life with Camille Oaks, and
fails to realize sufficiently that trouble lies ahead. Delicate
Mrs. Pritchard is not a strong mother. Unrealistic and
devious, she does not understand her daughter and
hides her own prudery and hate beneath socially ap-
proved mannerisms. No less obsessed than the female
religious figures in *The Grapes of Wrath,* Alice Chicoy
judges everything and everyone in her own shallow
terms. Fearful of approaching middle age and terrified by
the thought that Juan might leave her, she misjudges herself and others. She appears more concerned with flies
than with people, and treats Pimples with contempt. Why
Juan stays with her as long as he does is not clear.

While allegory serves to shape the actions and ideas of *The Wayward Bus,* the dominant structuring factors are the realistic materials themselves and principally the elements of plot. Plot here does not match the proportion and pace of *In Dubious Battle,* yet it appears more solidly based in the psychology of the characters, so that there are usually necessary and probable ties between feelings and motives on one hand and a character's actions on the other hand, just as there are such ties between the various actions. Material and sexual breakdowns or frustrations are the main influences on feelings, motives, and actions.

Essentials of the plot can be noted in three sequences of the novel. Chapters 1–6 provide a background history of Rebel Corners and accounts of morning activities as some characters resume familiar roles and others, the passengers, try to adjust to changed roles. The anxieties and discomforts caused by the bus breakdown disturb some but not all of the travelers. After a sleepless night, Alice is more bad-tempered than usual. Her largely sexual frustrations lead to tense scenes with Norma. Horton appears as chipper as ever, and Juan, who is proprietor as well as bus driver, is observant and calm. He repairs the bus, reassures Kit, pacifies Alice, and shrewdly judges the other characters. Material inconveniences test them, particularly the Pritchards and Van Brunt, who, lacking inner security, overreact to tensions and complications.

The scene of inconvenience, tension, and frustration at Rebel Corners is broken temporarily in chapter 7 as the action shifts to the Greyhound bus station in San Ysidro and the appearance of the shapely blonde who calls herself Camille Oaks. While hardly oblivious to bus travel discomforts, Camille does not let them bother her. Nor is she disturbed by the lustful reactions of Louie, the bus driver, or, at Rebel Corners, by the discerning eyes of Mildred. The attentions of Pritchard and Horton concern her, how-

ever, and they lead to consequences for the men. To prove
his worldliness, Pritchard tries to charm Camille, an act
his daughter finds distasteful and revealing. Reassured by
Camille's presence and disturbed by Alice's absence,
Norma has a scene with Alice and quits the job. Respond-
ing predictably, Alice begins her alcoholic journey as soon
as the bus journey begins. For the time Juan remains
imperturbable. But Van Brunt's complaints and arguments over the route prove irritating and contribute to
Juan's decision later to walk off.

In the last sequence, chapters 14–22, a few of the
characters accept life's burdens and frustrations and the
others show shaky values and motives. Juan Chicoy, torn
between duties to home and future, sensibly chooses present realities over future uncertainties. Having had her
fling and learned more about herself and her parents,
Mildred is ready to go on. She, too, is a realist. Although
Camille will not take any chances with Pritchard, she
may take them later with Ernest and Norma. Too tired
to decide, she "will see how it goes," the attitude, very
likely, of Ernest and the other realists as well. Norma
fights off Kit's sexual advances, but remains vulnerable to
future threats and frustrations. Kit, reliable as an assis-
tant, has much to learn about himself and women. But
he will survive. Van Brunt will not, and the Pritchards
face a very uncertain journey. Alice will return to life
when Juan returns to Rebel Corners. All in all, this postwar society is a mixture of the good, bad, and indifferent.

During the productive postwar years, Steinbeck expressed enthusiasm for a work that he believed would be
his best. Originally this was a story of his mother's people, the Hamiltons, who had left Ireland in the 1860s,
lived briefly in Connecticut, and then settled in California.
The account was to cover the 1860s to the early 1900s.
What eventually became *East of Eden* was first entitled
"Salinas Valley"; written in the first person, it began,

"Dear Tom and John: You are little boys now, when I am writing this." During the early writing another family appeared, the Trasks in Connecticut, who became so dominant that in the final 1951 version the Hamilton story is reduced and most of the first-person passages addressed to the sons have been eliminated.[7]

Despite such complications, Steinbeck remained determined and confident throughout the writing of the novel. "I think everything else I have written has been, in a sense, practice for this: . . . If *East of Eden* isn't good, then I've been wasting my time." [8] Five years of researching, writing, and rewriting went into the work. To fill in gaps in the Steinbeck family accounts of valley life, the writer read extensively in area newspapers, particularly in the *Salinas Californian*,[9] the hometown newspaper, and, for materials on the Bible, he obtained pertinent books and articles from his publisher. Since the new work was regarded as the *magnum opus*, Steinbeck pondered a number of points in depth.[10]

The most important point, which some critics believed had been avoided in earlier fiction, was the problem of evil, specifically the relationship of good and evil. This relationship, which is described in *East of Eden* as the main "story in the world," is expressed through the Genesis story of Cain and Abel, which, in turn, in the novel, is expressed through the characters and fates of the two families. In the early chapters, Adam Trask appears as a modern Abel and his half-brother Charles as Cain. Deeply jealous of the father's love of Adam and illustrating the biblical motif, Charles at one point nearly kills Adam. After the Civil War, Adam marries Cathy, a figure of evil. After they move to Salinas Valley, she has twin sons, one fathered seemingly by Charles. Deserting the family, she becomes the madam of a Salinas whorehouse. The two sons, Caleb and Aron, continue the Cain-Abel motif with various ramifications, including the death of Aron, the Abel figure.

As with *The Wayward Bus*, Steinbeck's hopes for a favorable reception and the critical success of *East of Eden* did not materialize. Despite good sales, critics as a rule found serious flaws in the characterizations, the thematic development, and the relating of the two families. Although there have been no dramatic reversals of critical views in the 1970s, strong support has appeared. One critic, Lester Marks, believes that the novel is Steinbeck's best, and Lawrence W. Jones, in his study of Steinbeck as fabulist, regards *East of Eden* as a "massive parable" and in various respects as a romance.[11]

To regard *East of Eden* as a romance, or as significantly romantic, is to make the same kind of critical realignment that appears necessary for a reevaluation of *The Wayward Bus*. Both novels rely upon allegorical materials, with the important general difference that realism is the central shaping influence and mode in *The Wayward Bus* and romanticism provides that influence and mode in *East of Eden*. The romanticism of *East of Eden* differs from that of *Cannery Row* in being more complex, pervasive, and affirmative. In its confident treatment of many topics and various aspects of the national identity, and in its expansiveness and variety of remarkable characters and actions, *East of Eden* resembles the nineteenth-century romance *Moby-Dick*.

Not restricted to a town area, as are *Tortilla Flat* and *Cannery Row*, or even to the broad geographical scope of *The Grapes of Wrath*, *East of Eden* covers not only the Salinas Valley region but also Washington, D.C., and areas in the country south, west, and north. The characters illustrate similar breadth and variety as we are given accounts of different families and a number of individual characters, several of whom are remarkable in that they reflect opposing moral views. Described as a "monster" of evil, Kate Trask, originally Cathy Ames, does not arise from a fictional society, but from the "subjective intensity" of an idea, reflecting the "suggestion of

allegory" that Northrop Frye finds characteristic of the
romance. Charles Trask, although a somewhat more realistic figure, nonetheless possesses a kind of single-minded-
ness that suggests allegorical simplification. Sam Hamilton
is a modern romantic whose dreams and achievements illustrate the inherent idealism and extravagance of the
romance.[12] Characters and actions alike in the novel appear larger and more intense than those of *The Wayward
Bus*.

Something of the romantic is perceptible also in the
general patterns in *East of Eden*. The novel does not have
the hour-by-hour, slow-moving plot of *The Wayward
Bus*. The patterns show instead a panoramic, confident
sweep from one region or topic or family to another
with a concentration on high points. As in Melville's
*Moby-Dick*, telling and explaining are often more important than showing. Lengthy expository and narrative materials are presented in a nineteenth-century manner,
sometimes in the form of essays on, for example, the
Trask brothers, Sam Hamilton's activities, and Cathy
Ames's maturation. The density of detail in such passages
underlines the exceptional nature of these characters.

The topics are wide-ranging, dealing with aspects of
nineteenth-century life, Civil War battles, Indian wars,
settlement of the West, power politics in Washington, and
town and country life in Connecticut. In the broad,
searching treatment, the Salinas area becomes both a
historical region and a symbolic landscape, a possible
American Eden, to which people travel great distances:
the Hamiltons from Ireland, the Trasks from Connecticut.
In this country, the journey becomes at times a quest, as
in Adam's flight to the great West and Sam's search for
ideals.

The division of *East of Eden* into four parts testifies
to both the sheer size of the work and the personal in-
volvement of the author, who begins three parts in the
first person. Such opening passages are not intrusive, as

some claim, but imaginative. The first-person essays suggest comparisons to some interchapters of *The Grapes of Wrath,* and also to first-person stances often found in romantic fiction.

In chapter 1, for example, Steinbeck as author-narrator provides a two-part, personal essay on the Valley. The chapter begins:

The Salinas Valley is . . . a long narrow swale between two ranges of mountains, and the Salinas River winds and twists up the center until it falls at last into Monterey Bay. . . . I remember that the Gabilan Mountains to the east of the valley were light gay mountains full of sun and loveliness and a kind of invitation.

The second part of the essay tells of settlements in the Valley, beginning with Indians, continuing with the greedy Spaniards, and culminating with the more aggressive and inventive Americans:

Then the Americans came—more greedy because there were more of them. They took the lands, remade the laws to make their titles good. And farmholds spread over the land, first in the valleys and then up the foothill slopes. . . . Wherever a trickle of water came out of the ground a house sprang up and a family began to grow and multiply. . . . And this is about the way the Salinas Valley was when my grandfather brought his wife and settled in the foothills to the east of King City.

The sense of a storyteller who is also an historian and a romantic pervades the passage.

Part Two begins with a shorter personal essay, a survey of the nineteenth century that prepares a context for the year 1900, the present time in chapter 12. It is an essay of lament, of tribute, and of regret that "strawberries will never taste so good again." Part Three begins with no such essay or introduction—why it does not is unclear. The essay for Part Four discusses reactions to death, in particular to the deaths of three prominent twentieth-century men. It also makes the point already referred to, namely, that the main story of the world is the relationship of good and evil: "We have only one story. All novels, all poetry, are built on the never-ending contest in ourselves of good and evil." The thematic materials of this essay balance the recollective and historical materials opening the novel. These essays, combining facts, themes, and symbols, strengthen the novel's overall unity, as well as the unity of each of the four parts.

To consider *East of Eden* as largely a romance is not to minimize, however, Steinbeck's problem in relating the Hamilton and Trask families. The problem remains, yet in some respects this relationship, too, is clarified and strengthened by romantic elements.

The families are related in Part One largely through thematic contrasts and juxtapositions: the energetic and idealistic Hamiltons in California and the gloomy, driven Trasks in the East; the dream-chasing Sam Hamilton and the opportunistic politician Cyrus. Such contrasts and ties clarify the broader themes of fatherhood, of filial love and rejection, and of good and evil.

The relating of the two families appears to be more organic in Part Two, where meetings of the two have consequences. The chief romantic figure in *East of Eden*, Sam Hamilton, appears in many chapters and comes to know the Trasks, whom he finds puzzling. At first stunned by Cathy's evil and then enraged by Adam's defeatism, Sam throttles the younger man and prevails upon him to name his sons and accept his own filial responsibilities. Adam does so. In perhaps the most powerful and significant scene in the novel, Sam Hamilton, Adam Trask, and Lee meet in Adam's living room to decide on names for the boys. After Sam reads from the Old Testament, they talk about their views of original sin, of Cain and Abel, and of human guilt and of people's rejection of one another. Appearing in the approximate center of *East of Eden*, this scene effectively illustrates a basic romantic idealism in both writer and characters: a belief in man's capacity to know and his ability to choose.

Steinbeck's broad, epic treatment does not, however, adequately control and relate family materials in Part Three. The Hamiltons, bearers of the romantic faith, play a diminished role as Sam, Lisa, and Una die in the early chapters and Tom and Dessie die in the closing ones. Adam Trask and his two sons assume greater prominence. The influence of Sam, however, is clearly evident in a scene before his death. Like the naming scene in Part Two, this scene in chapter 24 is near the middle of the novel; it develops motifs discussed in the previous scene and influences the direction of the action thereafter. Lee explains to Sam the discoveries of Chinese scholars who had studied Hebrew in the attempt to unravel the mysteries of the Cain and Abel story in Genesis. The scholars discovered a crucial difference between modern translations of the story and the original Hebrew version:

"Don't you see?" he cried. "The American Standard translation *orders* men to triumph over sin, and you can call sin ignorance. The King James translation makes a promise in "Thou shalt," meaning that men will surely triumph over sin. But the Hebrew word, the word *timshel*—"Thou mayest"—that gives a choice. It might be the most important word in the world. . . . That throws it right back on a man. For if 'Thou mayest'—it is also true that 'Thou mayest not.' Don't you see?" [13]

In this scene, Lee goes beyond Sam to become the pragmatic idealist, who, accepting the consequences of the search, will preach them to Adam and explain them to Caleb. Discussions in the scene broaden the thematic basis of the novel.

The romantic expansiveness in the earlier parts is subordinated to some extent in Part Four to a realistic treatment of theme and character as the Trasks leave the farm and move into the restrictive confines of town society. The emphases accordingly become more novelistic. Lee, who wisely returns to the family, provides not only moral guidance based in part on his new insights but also sound practical advice on raising boys and investing money. Adam, who loses much of his fortune in a business experiment, later rejects Cal and his gift of money. The complex Cal, in turn, rejects his brother Aron, an allegorical figure of good, who goes to his death because he is unable to face the cruel facts. After Adam's stroke, Lee studies brain pathology in order to understand and assist Adam, who finally chooses to forgive Cal.

As critics have pointed out, Steinbeck's treatment of the biblical motif and of evil is at times inconsistent.[14] Kate becomes more credible in Part Four; she deviates from her allegorical typing of evil by joining a church, developing a conscience, experiencing brief emotional reactions to Caleb and Aron, and, finally, by choosing to commit suicide. On the other hand, the more realistically portrayed Adam, who, Lee claims, could not help rejecting Caleb, later somewhat unexplainably summons the strength and understanding to forgive.

Although such inconsistencies and other flaws provide ample evidence that Steinbeck's hopes for another major work were not to be realized, *East of Eden* remains impressive. It shows a largeness of vision and treatment evident previously only in *The Grapes of Wrath*. If the insights into good and evil reveal no unusual depths or subtlety, they do show a complexity seldom evident in Steinbeck's earlier works. The problem of evil—oversimplified in earlier works, sometimes avoided, or often expressed in largely political terms—is examined in the discussions between Sam, Lee, and Adam, and in the motivations and fates of several figures, principally Cathy-Kate, Charles, and Caleb Trask. Affirmations of the good are effectively dramatized through Sam and Lee, the former an inventive dreamer, and the latter a hu-

manist who never loses faith in human dignity and rea-
son; and through the persistence of Adam and Cal, who,
despite odds, manage to illustrate that faith.

Although the novel's language lacks the vitality and
richness of prose found in *The Grapes of Wrath*, it is
usually equal to the demands the author places on it. *East
of Eden*, despite failures, not only deals with a wealth
of diverse materials but does so primarily through the
elusive and challenging forms of romance.

# 7

# Searches in the Last Years

After the publication of *East of Eden* in 1952, Steinbeck continued to write into the early 1960s but with uneven results. *Sweet Thursday* (1954), a sequel to *Cannery Row* (1945), is another narrative of Doc and Mack and the boys, along with Dora Flood's sister Fauna as Madame of the Bear Flag Restaurant, and Joseph and Mary Rivas as the new owners of Chong's grocery. Action centers on the efforts of Mack and others to find a suitable wife for Doc, who, back from the army, appears lonely and discontented. They find Suzy, one of Fauna's girls, and become entangled in a variety of skits culminating in the marriage of Doc and Suzy and with Doc as a contented professor at the California Institute of Technology. The comedy and slapstick reappear in a Rodgers and Hammerstein adaptation, *Pipe Dream* (1955). Neither novel nor play is regarded highly.

Based on Steinbeck's experiences in France in the mid-1950s and set in the near future, *The Short Reign of Pippin IV* (1957), also a musical-comedy fiction, tells of Pippin, a middle-aged astronomer turned king, who attempts to put into effect a national reform program. The reform measures are defeated. As portrayals of political groups and leaders in the course of the work rely more upon burlesque and less upon deft satire and wit, the exposé of modern political corruption becomes shrill.

. . .

A work of far greater importance occupied Steinbeck's time during these years. The lifelong interest in the King Arthur tales culminated in the late 1950s as he began his own translation of Malory's monumental work, *Morte d'Arthur*. To prepare thoroughly for the ambitious project, which began in 1956, Steinbeck spent a good deal of time in England, including a year and a half reading and taking notes on hundreds of books about the fifteenth century and about Malory. Through the years he had read and reread the Arthurian tales, first in the Caxton edition, including one he had received at age nine, and then in the 1947 edition of the Winchester manuscripts, which provides a considerably fuller treatment. Accompanied by his wife Elaine, who kept a photographic record, Steinbeck roamed the English and Welsh countryside, trying to gain a real sense of the land and its distant past and also of the figures and adventures of the tales.

He benefited also from talks with Eugène Vinaver, the world's foremost authority on Malory and the discoverer in 1936 of the Winchester manuscript. Impressed with an early translation by Steinbeck, Vinaver offered to assist the writer in any way possible. Predicting in 1959 that the actual translation of the entire work would take ten years, Steinbeck during this time regarded the project as "the largest and I hope the most important . . . I have undertaken." After the long and seemingly beneficial period of scholarly preparation, Steinbeck began writing in July 1958 and continued until October of the following year.[1]

In that time and perhaps during a short period in 1965, Steinbeck translated only part of the first volume of the projected two-volume work. The translation falls into two parts: first, five of the six parts of "The Tale of King Arthur"; and then, the "Gawain, Ewain, and Marhalt" section of the first romance and the entire "The

Noble Tale of Sir Launcelot of the Lake." These appeared
posthumously in *The Acts of King Arthur and His Noble
Knights* (1976).

Planning originally to remain close to "the rhythms
and tones of Malory," Steinbeck provides in the first five
sections a clear, readable translation that combines modern diction and phrasing and something of the texture of
Malory's language. In subsequent tales, taking more liber-
ties with the Winchester text edited by Vinaver, Steinbeck
makes cuts and elaborations designed to enhance the
dramatic qualities of the materials and to unify them
further. As befits the predilections of a modern novelist,
Steinbeck deepens characterizations through delineating
psychological qualities and also expands a three-page section of the adventures of Sir Ywain into thirty pages of
narrative which include a discussion of the long bow and
its effects on knighthood and government, as well as an
exposition of knightly codes and tournaments. The overall
mood and emphasis of the translation, however, remain
faithful to Malory. The beautifully wrought descriptions
of the West Country terrain in England provide a naturalistic setting for the adventures.

It is not clear why Steinbeck never completed the
translation. As his letters disclose, he lost enthusiasm for
the project, possibly because of complex and ambiguous
passages in the Malory text or because of the immense
problems of unifying the many tales and episodes. Had
Steinbeck lived and returned to the project, it would have
doubtless required an even greater expenditure of time
and effort than he had originally predicted. What we do
have has been well received, one scholar stating that if the
translation had been completed it "would probably have
become one of the standard works of our time." [3] The
present volume is valuable not only for the translations,
which deserve reading and study, but also for a brief
introduction by the writer and an appendix of seventy-

six letters written about the project from 1956 to 1965, most of them previously unpublished.

Steinbeck's disappointments over the Malory translations, a need to return to something else, and his impressions of America after returning from England in 1959 may have led to *The Winter of Our Discontent* (1961), a satiric portrayal of Americans and their values in 1960. Newspaper articles in late 1959 and the writer's observations of conditions on the East Coast convinced him that many things had gone wrong in the country. Writing to close friends, he expressed deep concern over what appeared to be widespread violence, cruelty, and hypocrisy —"symptoms of a general immorality which pervades every level of our national life" (he cited the TV scandals of the time)—and the difficulty of raising children properly in such an environment.[4] These concerns would be expressed at length in his last novel.

*The Winter of Our Discontent* differs from *The Wayward Bus*, another and earlier examination of American foibles, in that the locale is not western, the time is some twelve years later, the national situation has changed, and—a real innovation for a Steinbeck novel— the story is told in the first-person voice. The narrator is Ethan Allen Hawley, a descendant of Puritans, a former World War II infantry captain, a Harvard graduate, and a married man, father of two teenage children. He is also a clerk in a store that he had once owned but lost through bankruptcy.

The novel begins on Good Friday. During the day, Ethan talks successively with a bank teller, the town banker, an attractive divorcee named Margie Young-Hunt, and with Marullo, the store owner. He also turns down a bribe from a salesman. In bed that night Ethan thinks of his ancestors and of Danny Taylor, the town drunk and a lifelong friend. On Saturday the teller, Joe Morphy, tells him that he should have accepted the bribe, and

Margie predicts a change in his fortunes. After talking
on Easter Sunday with Mr. Baker, the banker, and with
Marullo, Hawley decides to feather his own nest and succeeds in finagling the store from Marullo and valuable
land from Taylor. A potentially big man in the community, Hawley discovers much too late that his son had
cheated in a national essay contest. Distressed by such
developments, Hawley attempts suicide but stops short
because of a reminder of his honest, idealistic daughter.

In narrating the intricate course of events leading to
the attempted suicide, Hawley necessarily concentrates on
New Baytown, Long Island, "one of the first clear and
defined whole towns in America," and also one of the most
thoroughly explored towns in Steinbeck's fiction. Since the
Hawleys have lived in New Baytown for generations, the
narrator knows the town thoroughly. Too poor to own a
car, Ethan walks to work each day and on sleepless nights
sometimes saunters around the town, providing as he goes
a verbal map of streets, buildings, and the Old Harbor,
where once whalers and men enlivened the seafront scene.
Hawley provides also a history, explaining that the first
settlers

successfully combined piracy and puritanism, which aren't
so unalike when you come right down to it. Both had a
strong dislike for opposition and both had a roving eye for
other people's property. Where they merged, they produced a
hard-bitten, surviving bunch of monkeys. I know about them
because my father made me know. He was a kind of high
amateur ancestor man and I've always noticed that ancestor
people usually lack the qualities of the ones they celebrate.

During the whaling era, New Baytown flourished. As
whaling declined in the late nineteenth century, however,
the town fell behind nearby settlements that continued to
grow and prosper in the twentieth century. Baytown resi-
dents in 1960 still seem to prefer the old ways, disliking
the prospect of the bustle and noise of a large tourist port.

Others, however, like Mr. Baker, want the town to keep up with the times, expand, build an airport, and take advantage of tourist and other business opportunities. The split in community views is one basis for discontent in the town and also in its chief historian and spokesman.

The town families, which reflect the divided aspirations and moral conflicts, appear almost as essential to the novel as the Joads, Wilsons, and others are to *The Grapes of Wrath*. The Hawleys, Phillipses, Eggars, Bakers, and Taylors in the later work go back for generations. The Hawleys are no longer prominent and the Taylors, represented by Danny, who was dismissed from the Naval Academy in World War II, have all but died out. The Bakers, however, headed by the town banker, remain powerful in the community. Although the Alfio Marullo family is a relatively new addition to New Baytown, the family name, as Marullo informs Hawley, who had referred proudly to his own family history, goes back "maybe two, three thousand years. Marullus is from Rome, Valerius Maximus tells about it. What's two hundred years?" The family's longevity is apparently a vital factor in the formation of Marullo's integrity.

As a family the Hawleys exist as much in the past as in the present. At least that would be the narrator's view. He loves his wife, admires her household efficiency and dedication, but regards her as overly practical and unconcerned with the life of the mind. Although the teenage son, Allen, has a few good qualities, he is nonetheless overbearing, opinionated, and quick to rationalize any form of apathy or dishonesty. Only Ellen, in Hawley's mind, represents staunch moral qualities of the past. Not only is she comparatively mature and thoughtful, but she is honest as well. Her love of the family talisman, a translucent stone brought back perhaps from China by an ancestor, indicates her sensitive awareness of the family's past.

Hawley is often preoccupied with that past. Sometimes he thinks of his father, a kind, gentle man, whom
he loved but cannot admire because his weaknesses and
foolish investments cost the family its fortune and indirectly led to Ethan's bankruptcy after World War II.
An insecure man himself, Ethan Hawley thinks fondly of
the great-aunt Deborah and his grandfather, who represent the strength and moral tradition of the family. The
grandfather taught the young Ethan about ships and informed him of the facts behind the burning of the *Belle
Adair;* more important, the old man's strength of character and sense of moral duty continue to provide guide
lights to Ethan in difficult times. His great-aunt, who was
more imaginative and aware of evil, also serves Hawley
as a moral guide. Speaking out of the past in parables
about duty and evil, she represents the necessity for a
strict, practical accounting. The ancestors and their
preachments grow vague for the narrator, however, if he
is acting or thinking in terms they would not condone.

Other areas of community life, particularly the local
government and business sector, are targets of Steinbeck's
satire. The night watchman—who starts many a harmful
rumor—the judges, the town manager, and the council
are all morally culpable. Stonewall Jackson Smith, the
chief of police, however, is as straight and hard as a die.
Such a division between the immoral and moral, the self-
serving and dutiful, appears also in major characters who
highlight the decline since the days of the heroic past.
The efficient Joe Morphy is honest in bank affairs, but he
is always willing to jump into bed with Margie Young-
Hunt, and sees nothing wrong in accepting the Biggers bribe. Biggers, a slick operator, willing to recognize
Hawley's unexpected finesse, is another indicator of the
subtlety with which money and greed corrupt morality.
The town's leading citizen, Mr. Baker, adroitly combines
the piratical and puritanic dispositions of his ancestors.

Gentlemanly and well-mannered, scrupulous in administering bank affairs, Baker is first in the community for covert operations.

That Baker remains first until outmanuevered by the town historian dramatizes the extent of both community and individual failings. Steinbeck's general plan for revealing these appears sound; his tactics, however, are questionable. Hawley's reasons for desiring changes are clear enough: the wife and family deserve a car, TV, and other material improvements; a Harvard graduate and war hero deserves a better position; Hawley's ancestors, with some exceptions, watched out for number one; many in the town do, too. Hawley proceeds to do so. This is fairly convincing because years of servitude and resignation have made Hawley an inner-directed man. A great person for verbal comedy, witty sermons for shelves of groceries, and endless silly names for his wife, Hawley regards planning the bank job as a game and betraying Marullo or Taylor as mental processes that can be controlled. When he discovers that he cannot do so, the entire matter has become too absorbing for him to stop.

Descriptions of the process are interesting because Hawley's mind is involuted and his journey into that mind is revealing. Steinbeck's accounts of the journey skillfully, sometimes deeply, illuminate rationalizations, decisions, and doubts. These accounts, however, do not demonstrate consistently that even a frustrated and morally confused and vulnerable character like Ethan Allen Hawley would, in a few months, desert a lifetime of moral responsibility and betray family and friends in order to show at last the piratical rather than the puritanic dispositions of his inheritance.

Perhaps to shore up such weak points and to universalize the plot, Steinbeck includes mythical materials, which are usually inverted. Hawley, with his religious sensibilities, begins as a Christ-like figure, who, on Good Friday, rejects a money bribe and temptation of the flesh.

On Easter Sunday, deciding to betray Marullo and Taylor
and rob the bank, he assumes Judas qualities. While
these and other inverted allusions clarify and enrich the
plot they do not strengthen the narrator's motives. The
political myths, centering around the national "I Love
America" contest and July Fourth celebration, are in a
sense inverted by the town scandals, Allen's plagarism,
and Hawley's own political future. The references and
parallels to *Richard III* are likewise satiric, for the king,
whose schemes and betrayals provide a backdrop for
Hawley's, is bold and courageous as well as subtle, and is
involved in mighty, far-reaching actions.[5] Hawley takes
bold steps and is sometimes subtle, but his betrayals of
Marullo and Danny are cowardly and he is not involved
in heroic or tragic undertakings.

After many years of living in New York City and
Sag Harbor and several years abroad working on the
Malory project, Steinbeck realized that he had lost touch
with the country. With *The Winter of Our Discontent*
completed, he decided to regain that contact through a
round-the-country trip. He ordered a powerful, three-
quarter ton pickup with a cabin attached, named it
Rocinante, carefully stocked the vehicle with abundant
provisions, and, with his French poodle alongside, started
out after Labor Day, 1960, driving counterclockwise from
the East. The account of his experiences, *Travels with
Charley in Search of America* (1962), resembles *Sea of
Cortez* (1940) in that both center on a long journey, a
search for facts and ideas, and both are essentially nonfictional first-person narratives. *Travels with Charley* differs in that it is not intended to be scientific, poetic, or
speculative, and it is clearly not a collaboration. The book
is, quite simply, a relaxed, episodic account of one man's
travels in his native land.

The travels cover many of the fifty states; they take
Steinbeck and his dog through countless towns and vil-

lages and occasionally a big city. No attempt is made to provide equal coverage for each part of the country, and he admits that "in the dog-leg of Virginia . . . my journey went away and left me stranded far from home." But generally the descriptions of the country's variety, size, and complexity are well paced and absorbing.

Unifying the accounts is the implied presence of a humane, sometimes angered observer, who is also a story-teller with an easy sense of humor. Evocations of scenes— a roadside cafe, a gas station, campgrounds—are factual and realistic. The people—Steinbeck informs the reader that he never met a stranger—are portrayed with a practiced hand: a shy young boy who wants to know if he can go along on the trip; a ranch caretaker who relents and lets Steinbeck camp overnight; a New York cop who redirects his route. Many incidents resemble excerpts from a realistic novel. Speech and conversation are faithfully portrayed even though, as Steinbeck explains, he found no "truly local" speech until he reached Montana.

For a change of pace, there are one-way talk fests with Charley, a curious, forward creature, whose involvements with other dogs or with their owners provide opportunities for Steinbeck to comment as he wishes. The writing itself is generally adequate. There are occasional touches of the sentimental, but years of experience and a toughened sensibility help keep the portrayal of Americans and their activities in perspective.

As *Travels with Charley* is not a nonteleological study, the writer is not hesitant in advancing opinions. There is frequent criticism of the national emphasis upon the big, the efficient, and the "modern." Steinbeck avoided superhighways, national parks, and splendid motels, was amused by and skeptical of fast-serve and efficient restaurants and other eateries, and in many places decried other signs of progress, big government, and the "frantic bustle of America." Many people encountered in his trip appeared indifferent toward their jobs, their ways of life, and the country in general. Loneliness, greed, and apathy identified successes as well as failures. At one point Steinbeck concludes that discontent may underlie the widespread desire of his countrymen to travel, which may be as typically American as the desire to stay put.

*Travels with Charley* does not, however, present a "wasteland vision," or evidence supporting one, as has been claimed.[6] Even apart from Steinbeck's well-known compassion and love of country, which would tend to moderate his own criticism, the prevailing objective impression is that American life, despite its weaknesses and excesses, will endure. The country is sound because its people are essentially unified. Despite differences in economic status, religion, race, and national background, Americans resemble each other:

This is not patriotic whoop-de-do; it is carefully observed fact. It is a fact that Americans from all sections and of all racial extractions are more alike than the Welsh are like the English, the Lancashireman like the Cockney, or for that matter the Lowland Scot like the Highlander. It is astonishing that this has happened in less than two hundred years and most of it in the last fifty. The American identity is an exact and provable thing.

During the many stops around the country Steinbeck is impressed also by natives who show common sense, tolerance, courage, and adaptability.

A number of such individuals are described at length. The descriptions, set pieces that provide a loose structural pattern in *Travels with Charley*, present to us a New England minister in a John Knox church, who "spoke of hell as an expert, not the mush-mush hell of these soft days, but a well-stoked, white-hot hell served by technicians of the first order"; an actor in the Dakotas, also traveling with only a dog, who earned his livelihood by appearing before schools, churches, and social groups, wherever more than three people gathered together; a giant in an Oregon gas station who took time to locate badly needed tires for the writer by calling places in and out of town and even involving his brother-in-law in the search; a young Amarillo veterinarian who, unlike an incompetent colleague in Spokane, was pleasant, efficient, and restored Charley to perfect health in a few days. Perhaps the most distinguished individual commemorated in Steinbeck's travel record is an elderly gentleman: Monsieur Ci Git, originally of St. Louis, whose gentleness, intelligence, and concern for others Steinbeck found heartwarming and reassuring after the racial outbursts of a New Orleans group encountered several hours earlier.

Steinbeck's last assessment of the country is made in *America and Americans* (1966). Believing that only foreigners had previously written such studies, he confidently proposed as a "blowed-in-the-glass American" to write one. The result is an informative collection of nine essays, beginning with "E Pluribus Unum," which describes the different nationalities that helped make the country, and ending with "Americans and the Future," which evaluates our weaknesses, morals, and hopes for the future. Other essays include "Paradox and Dream," an exploration of national differences and the great and little American dreams; "Government of the People," a discussion of nominating conventions, the presidency, and Congress; and "Genus Americanus," the longest essay, a spirited examination of classes in a classless society. Included in the folio-sized volume are many full-page photographs by nationally recognized photographers, which illustrate in a general manner essay topics and contribute an impression of the country's variety, complexity, and greatness.

Making no claim to objectivity or to a scholarly approach, Steinbeck states at the beginning that "this is a book of opinions, unashamed and individual. . . . What else could it be?" Steinbeck's statement is to be taken literally. The essays provide frank, serious, often harsh comment on the difficulties of minorities, on inept presidents and dirty politics, on mistreatment of the land, women, and children, and on the increasing devotion to wealth, material possessions, and status. The plight of blacks is examined in "Created Equal," which ends: "We will not have overcome the trauma . . . [of] slavery . . . until we cannot remember whether the man we just spoke to in the street was Negro or white." Other essays examine ways in which the country and its people have failed to live up to traditional dreams and ideals.

Like *Travels with Charley*, this book demonstrates the writer's dogged faith in Americans and his recognition of their strengths and weaknesses. The idealistic beliefs, which provide guidelines in most of the fiction, including the pessimistic *The Winter of Our Discontent*, appear in diminished form throughout the volume and balance the pessimistic assessments. Steinbeck finds much in the American character and achievement to be thankful for. The last essay concludes: "Our experience in America has endowed us for the change that is coming. We have never sat still for long; we have never been content with a place, a building—or with ourselves."

Although *America and Americans* abounds in national myths and symbols, especially political and moral, it is not a work in which the literary use of myth, symbol, figurative language, or character study are central concerns. As in *Travels with Charley*, the novelistic skills are evident in accounts of people—for example, the woman in New York City who one summer appeared daily on the sidewalk with a table, chair, and beach umbrella and proceeded to relax and enjoy the scene—and in narrative passages such as the commentary on American presidents or on typical homes.

The essays are unified by related topics and by the familiar tone and manner of a brilliant writer, who, in writing of the country, reveals something of his own

shortcomings and strengths. The book lacks the brilliance
of his best work. It is at times superficial and because of
the scope it leaves much unsaid. But generally the opinions are well informed, advanced with confidence, and
illustrated with examples culled from many years of acute
and sympathetic observation. As one expression of a
man's love of his country and his skeptical hopes for it,
this last work by John Steinbeck is a fitting testimony.

# 8

# A Conclusion

Literary historians may have difficulty in placing John Steinbeck and his work because neither belongs convincingly with a recognized trend or group. Developing as a writer about the same time as Fitzgerald, Dos Passos, Faulkner, and Hemingway—all born around the turn of the century—he appears separate from them in various ways. Unlike these writers, Steinbeck was not powerfully influenced by World War I; and unlike them and others he was not among the expatriates writing from Paris in the 1920s about the predicaments of Americans in Europe and at home.

Along with such writers as John Dos Passos and James T. Farrell, Steinbeck has been considered a social-protest writer of the 1930s. *In Dubious Battle, Of Mice and Men,* and *The Grapes of Wrath* strongly criticize economic injustices and particularly the plight of the have-nots. Yet the generic hallmarks of social-protest fiction—a revolutionary message, and characters and actions designed to express that message—rarely appear. The 1930s fiction and other works by Steinbeck have been described also as realistic or naturalistic, familiar terms for dominant literary trends or groups in those years. However, Steinbeck's fiction resists such categories, for in *The Grapes of Wrath* the realism is enriched by a poetic language and by concerns with the mystical aspects of the biological. The naturalistic emphases, which are some-

times as severe as those of Dos Passos, are moderated in
that novel and in *Of Mice and Men* by down-to-earth
humor and compassion. The man and his work may be
regarded as western—possibly the most apt of these
descriptions—until one thinks of various fictions and
nonfictions that are not western and of others like *Tortilla
Flat* and *Cannery Row* that appear to be western, but do
not deal with such primary concerns as space, the land
and nature, and man's place in them.

The nature and direction of Steinbeck's fiction may
be understood more clearly if approached through characteristic symbols and themes, such as the tide-pool image
cited by Fontenrose.[1] The family is another important
symbol, often at the center of the dramatic forces of a
story or novel and illustrating human strengths and
weaknesses. Dangers of nature and society disrupt the
Torres family in "Flight," and the thoughtless machinations of the Munroes scatter several families in *The Pastures of Heaven*. Violence, abnormality, or eccentricity
illustrate the vulnerability of man and family in the fates
of the Battles, Van Deventers, and Maltbys in that novel,
and the Nolans in *In Dubious Battle*. The Joads in *The
Grapes of Wrath* manage to survive economic and natural
upheavals, but at the end must recognize the emergence
of a larger family. There are stable families in the fiction,
including, along with the Joads, Wilsons, and Wain-
wrights in *The Grapes of Wrath*, the Whitesides in *The
Pastures of Heaven*, and the Hamiltons, who, in *East of
Eden*, finding little of value in the ranch land, find
strength within themselves. A few families appear contented: the Tiflins in *The Red Pony*, and, until the father
becomes overly ambitious, the Kinos in *The Pearl*.

Territory and social protest are two other identifying
marks of the fiction. Central California—most memorably
Monterey and several valleys—and the area near Sallisaw, Oklahoma, may appear less familiar to readers than
Frenchman's Bend, Jefferson, and the farms of Faulk-

ner's Yoknapatawpha county, yet the Steinbeck treatment
of land is nonetheless remarkable for its acute and graphic
portrayal of environment and of the effects of nature on
man. It is remarkable as well for an early and brilliant
study of the predicaments of the small farmer and migrant worker confronted by the powerful alignment of big
farmers and finance—a confrontation that persists into
the 1970s. Social protest, a *sine qua non* in many of Steinbeck's novels, figures significantly in the satiric realism
of *The Wayward Bus* and in a more subtle form in *The
Winter of our Discontent,* as well as in the tougher-
grained novels of the 1930s.

Instrumental in shaping such elements and the fictions themselves is Steinbeck's moral vision which has
been variously described, interpreted, praised, and ques-
tioned through the years. Steinbeck's pervasive compassion for human beings appears most characteristically in
portrayals of the most vulnerable: the naive, handicapped,
and disenfranchised—the Maltbys, Danny and the paisanos, George and Lennie—who rarely find the promised land, at least not as they dream of it. Tolerance and
sympathy are evident also in the complicated predicaments of Elisa, Doc of *Cannery Row,* Juan Chicoy, and
Adam Trask. The fundamentally affirmative quality of the
vision, however, tends on the one hand to minimize
complexities and shadings of modern life, particularly in
ethical values or choices, and on the other hand, to reveal more of group characteristics and ideas than of an
individual's heart and mind. This is in keeping with the
strong idealistic and intuitive elements in the vision. Major
characters such as Danny, Jim Nolan, Tom Joad, and Sam
Hamilton, whose feelings and motives are rarely probed
in psychological depth, tend to lose concreteness as the
novel's end approaches; they gradually become vague
embodiments of social and economic views.

The literary craftsmanship and skill with which the
themes, symbols, and moral vision are expressed would

seem to identify most definitely Steinbeck's fiction and
ensure his place with the best writers of his generation.
With them he shared a ceaseless dedication to mastering
the art of fiction. "The Chrysanthemums," "Flight," and
*Of Mice and Men* are distinguished for precision, clarity,
and sensitivity of language and for economy and proportion of form. Characters in these and other works illustrate a versatility of execution from the minutely realistic Jody Tiflin, to a variety of allegorical figures in many
of the fictions, to the symbolic realism of Ma Joad and
Juan Chicoy, to the complicated and introspective narrator, Ethan Allen Hawley. No less effectively at times than
Fitzgerald and Hemingway, Steinbeck experimented with
nuances of dialogue and prose style and with varieties of
point of view; and in diversity of works if not in richness
he may have equalled Faulkner, creating not only
stories and novels but also parables, plays, novel-plays,
and nonfiction, among the latter being the superb *Sea of
Cortez*, written with Ed Ricketts.

Steinbeck's own views of writing, and of his principles and goals as a writer, can serve to clarify the man
and his work. In the Nobel Prize acceptance speech of
1962, Steinbeck elaborates on what he describes as the
"high duties and the responsibilities of the makers of literature." Accepting the prize with humility but also with
confidence and pride, Steinbeck makes clear that literature is not written by the few for the few; nor is it
meant for the contemplation of that modern preoccupation, "universal fear." Through the ages literature has
been created by writers who "are not separate and
exclusive" and who strive to deepen understanding and
to resolve fears of the heart and spirit:

This is not new. The ancient commission of the writer has
not changed. He is charged with exposing our many grievous
faults and failures, with dredging up to the light our dark
and dangerous dreams for the purpose of improvement.

Furthermore, the writer is delegated to declare and to

celebrate man's proven capacity for greatness of heart and spirit—for gallantry in defeat—for courage, compassion and love. In the endless war against weakness and despair, these are the bright rally-flags of hope and of emulation.

I hold that a writer who does not passionately believe in the perfectibility of man, has no dedication nor any membership in literature.[2]

Steinbeck's best works brilliantly expose mankind's "grievous faults and failures," alert us to social and economic dangers, and remind us of our forgotten commitments and dreams. Steinbeck's strongest convictions and passions appear in his fundamental belief in humanity, in his expectation that man will endure, and that the creative forces of the human spirit will prevail.

# Notes

## 1. THE MAN AND HIS WORK

1. Warren French, *John Steinbeck*, rev. ed. (Boston, 1975), p. 34.
2. Elaine Steinbeck and Robert Wallsten, eds. *Steinbeck: A Life in Letters* (New York, 1975), p. 527.
3. Ibid., p. 758.
4. Nelson Valjean, *John Steinbeck, The Errant Knight: An Intimate Biography of His California Years* (San Francisco, 1975), pp. 29–31; Joseph Fontenrose, *John Steinbeck: An Introduction and Interpretation* (New York, 1963), pp. 1–2.
5. Valjean, *Steinbeck*, pp. 24–25. Martha Heasley Cox, "In Search of John Steinbeck: His People and His Land," *San Jose Studies* 1 (Nov., 1975), 41–60, has also been informative.
6. Valjean, *Steinbeck*, pp. 32, 39; Cox, "In Search," 45–48; Peter Lisca, "John Steinbeck: A Literary Biography," in *Steinbeck and His Critics: A Record of Twenty-Five Years*, ed. E. W. Tedlock, Jr., and C. V. Wicker (Albuquerque, N.M., 1957), pp. 3–5.
7. Valjean, *Steinbeck*, pp. 35–36.
8. Ibid., p. 28; Cox, "In Search," pp. 45–49.
9. Valjean, *Steinbeck*, pp. 43–44.
10. Peter Lisca, *The Wide World of John Steinbeck* (New Brunswick, N.J., 1958), p. 24.
11. Valjean, *Steinbeck*, pp. 42–47, 62–64, 81–85, 89–94.
12. Ibid., p. 107.

13. Richard Astro, "John Steinbeck: A Biographical Portrait," in *John Steinbeck: A Dictionary of His Fictional Characters*, ed. T. Hayashi (Metuchen, N.J., 1976), pp. 5–6; Valjean, *Steinbeck*, pp. 136–37.
14. Astro, "John Steinbeck," pp. 3–4.
15. Jackson J. Benson, " 'To Tom, Who Lived It': John Steinbeck and the Man from Weedpatch," *Journal of Modern Literature* 5 (April, 1976), 151–94. *L'Affaire Lettuceburg*, alternately titled "Oklahoma" and "Lettuceberg," was a 60,000 word manuscript that Steinbeck discarded. See Lisca, *The Wide World*, pp. 147–8.
16. Lisca, *The Wide World*, pp. 183–6; Astro, "John Steinbeck," pp. 13–14.
17. French, *John Steinbeck* (rev. ed.), p. 30.
18. Ibid., pp. 31–33.
19. Steinbeck and Wallsten, *Steinbeck: A Life in Letters*, pp. 694–7; Astro, "John Steinbeck," p. 20.

## 2. THE STEINBECK TERRITORY—
### COMMITMENTS AND CONFLICTS

1. Martha Heasley Cox, "In Search of John Steinbeck: His People and His Land," *San Jose Studies* 1 (Nov., 1975), 41–60, has been informative on places and names. Jackson J. Benson, "Environment as Meaning: John Steinbeck and the Great Central Valley," *Steinbeck Quarterly* 10 (Winter, 1977), 12–20, has provided similar information and clarified the general idea of environment in Steinbeck's work; see in particular pp. 12–13.
2. Peter Lisca, *The Wide World of John Steinbeck* (New Brunswick, N.J., 1958), pp. 98–100. John Ditsky, "Steinbeck's 'Flight': The Ambiguity of Manhood," *Steinbeck Quarterly* 5 (Summer-Fall, 1972), 83–84.
3. According to the interpretation, allegorical emphases in the fiction can be regarded as a strength or as a weakness. See, for example, Lawrence C. Jones, *John Steinbeck as Fabulist*, ed. M. LaFrance (*Steinbeck Monograph Series*, No. 3, 1973), pp. 3–34; and Howard

Levant, *The Novels of John Steinbeck: A Critical Study* (Columbia, Mo., 1974), pp. 234–289.

4. Quoted by Lisca, *The Wide World*, pp. 56–57.
5. See, for example, Warren French, *John Steinbeck* (New York, 1961), pp. 41–42. Richard Peterson, *"The Pastures of Heaven,"* in *A Study Guide to Steinbeck: A Handbook to His Major Works*, ed. T. Hayashi (Metuchen, N.J., 1974), pp. 88, 97.
6. French, *John Steinbeck*, pp. 43–44.
7. My views of groups in Steinbeck's work have been clarified through Lisca, *The Wide World*, pp. 64–70 and through Peterson, pp. 99–101.
8. Peterson, "The Pastures," p. 100.
9. Lisca, *The Wide World*, pp. 74–75, 75–77.
10. Joseph Fontenrose, *John Steinbeck: An Introduction and Interpretation* (New York, 1963), pp. 35–40.
11. See, for example, Lisca, *The Wide World*, p. 79, and in particular Stanley Alexander, "The Conflict of Form in *Tortilla Flat*," *American Literature* 40 (March, 1968), 58–60.

## 3.   Conflicts and Searches in the 1930s

1. Freeman Champney, "John Steinbeck, Californian," in *Steinbeck and His Critics: A Record of Twenty-Five Years*, E. W. Tedlock, Jr., and C. V. Wicker (Albuquerque, N.M., 1957), p. 138.
2. Peter Lisca, *The Wide World of John Steinbeck* (New Brunswick, N.J., 1958), p. 110. Lisca quotes a passage from Champney describing the Salinas strike scene, pp. 109–110.
3. Lisca, pp. 112–13; Jackson J. Benson, " 'To Tom Who Lived It': John Steinbeck and the Man from Weedpatch," *Journal of Modern Literature* 5 (April, 1976), 173.
4. Quoted by Betty L. Perez, "Steinbeck's *In Dubious Battle*" (1936), in *A Study Guide to Steinbeck: A Handbook to his Major Works*, ed. T. Hayashi (Metuchen, N.J., 1974), p. 48.

5. Lisca, *The Wide World*, p. 113.

6. Daniel Aaron, *Writers on the Left* (New York, 1961), pp. 325, 399.

7. Warren French, *John Steinbeck* (New York, 1961), provides an enlightening interpretation of Steinbeck's reliance on and use of Arthurian materials. See, for example, pp. 62–71, "Parsifal's Last Stand." Joseph Fontenrose, *John Steinbeck: An Introduction and Interpretation* (New York, 1963), pp. 46–53. Howard Levant, *The Novels of John Steinbeck: A Critical Study* (Columbia, Mo., 1974), at one point describes the novel as "a moral fable, a study of good and evil," p. 77.

8. Walter B. Rideout, *The Radical Novel in the United States, 1900–1954: Some Interrelations of Literature and Society* (New York, 1956), p. 325. Various critics of the 1930s regarded the working-class background of the author as another fundamental, but Rideout's detailed discussion indicates that there is no consensus on this view. See pp. 165–70.

9. Warren French, in *John Steinbeck* (New York, 1961), p. 62, states, for example, that *In Dubious Battle* is not mainly about a strike.

10. Lisca, *The Wide World*, pp. 110–11.

11. The dream, the friendship of George and Lennie, and the characters have Arthurian overtones. See French, pp. 72–74, who believes that this is Steinbeck's last novel to be influenced by the legends.

12. Lisca, *The Wide World*, p. 139.

4.   AFFIRMATION AND PROTEST IN THE WEST

1. Warren French, ed., *A Companion to The Grapes of Wrath* (New York, 1963), pp. 105–6, provides information on background and reception of the novel. See also Peter Lisca, *The Wide World of John Steinbeck* (New Brunswick, N.J., 1958), pp. 144–51.

2. Martin Staples Shockley, "The Reception of *The Grapes of Wrath* in Oklahoma," in French, *A Companion*, pp. 117–18.

3. French, *A Companion*, pp. 109, 110–15.

4. Ibid., p. 116.

5. Joseph Fontenrose, *John Steinbeck: An Introduction and Interpretation* (New York, 1963), pp. 75–82. See also H. Kelly Crockett, "The Bible and *The Grapes of Wrath*," *College English* 24 (Dec., 1962), 193–98; Martin S. Shockley, "Christian Symbolism in *The Grapes of Wrath*," *College English* 18 (Nov., 1956), 87–90.

6. See Lisca, *The Wide World*, pp. 160–65.

7. Ibid., pp. 157, 161–62.

8. While Steinbeck's tendency toward abstractness or allegory can lead to sentimentality, it may also complicate a characterization or situation by indicating a variety of possibilities. Characters in *Tortilla Flat*, for example, are not as simplistic as they might appear: they are parasites as well as individualists; as such they illustrate various ideas. The situation of the Joads has its sentimental possibilities, for clearly they are victimized by both nature and economics. But they are also victimized by their own failures with the land and their obvious failures within the family itself. At the same time they possess various sound qualities.

9. See F. I. Carpenter, "John Steinbeck: The Philosophical Joads," *College English* 2 (Jan., 1941), 315–25; and also Eric W. Carlson, "Symbolism in *The Grapes of Wrath*," *College English* 19 (Jan., 1958), 172–75.

10. Chester E. Eisinger, "Jeffersonian Agrarianism in *The Grapes of Wrath*," *University of Kansas City Review* 14 (Autumn, 1947), 149–54.

11. French, *A Companion*, p. 33. The article is reprinted by French, pp. 31–42.

12. *The Grapes of Wrath, Text and Criticism*, ed. Peter Lisca (New York, 1972), p. xiv, contains a helpful map and an itinerary of the Joads. Jackson J. Benson, "Environment as Meaning: John Steinbeck and the Great Central Valley," *Steinbeck Quarterly* 10 (Winter, 1977), 13–17, describes the Valley in detail and regards it for the Joads as a "limbo," "hell," "reverse Eden." In " 'To Tom, Who Lived It': John Steinbeck

and the Man from Weedpatch," *Journal of Modern Literature* 5 (April, 1976), 151–210, Benson explains that Steinbeck never made the trip from Oklahoma with any real-life Joads, and he describes in detail a minor government official in charge of camps, and Steinbeck's travels with him in the Valley.

13. See, for example, Howard Levant, *The Novels of John Steinbeck: A Critical Study* (Columbia, Mo., 1974), pp. 112–29.

14. For helpful studies of women characters, see *Steinbeck's Women: Essays in Criticism*, ed. Tetsumaro Hayashi (Steinbeck Monograph Series, No. 9, 1979).

15. For different interpretations of this scene, see Fontenrose, *John Steinbeck*, p. 81; Lisca, *The Wide World*, pp. 173–74; Howard Levant, *The Novels of John Steinbeck*, pp. 122–23.

16. This scene, too, has defenders as well as critics. See, for example, Peter Lisca, "The Dynamics of Community in *The Grapes of Wrath*," in *From Irving to Steinbeck: Studies of American Literature in Honor of Harry R. Warfel*, ed. M. Deakin and P. Lisca (Gainesville, Fla., 1972), p. 140; and Levant, *The Novels*, pp. 124–25.


## 5.  WARTIME HEROES AND COMMUNITIES

1. Peter Lisca, *The Wide World of John Steinbeck* (New Brunswick, N.J., 1958), pp. 178–180; Richard Astro, "Steinbeck's *Sea of Cortez*" in *A Study Guide to Steinbeck: A Handbook to His Major Works*, ed. T. Hayashi (Metuchen, N.J., 1974), p. 170.

2. Astro, "Steinbeck's *Sea*," pp. 173–5.

3. Ibid., p. 177.

4. See in particular, Richard Astro, *John Steinbeck and Edward F. Ricketts: The Shaping of a Novelist* (Minneapolis, 1973), pp. 14, 24, 27, 37–39. Joseph Fontenrose, *John Steinbeck: An Introduction and Interpretation* (New York, 1963), pp. 91–92.

5. See Astro, *Steinbeck and Ricketts*, pp. 31–33, and Fontenrose, *John Steinbeck*, pp. 89–90.

6.  Lisca, *The Wide World*, pp. 186–87.

7.  Lawrence W. Jones, "Poison in the Cream Puff: The Human Condition in *Cannery Row*," ed. M. LaFrance, *Steinbeck Society* 7 (Spring, 1974), 35–40, discusses romantic aspects of the novel.

8.  Lisca, *The Wide World*, p. 198.

### 6.  POSTWAR ALLEGORY, REALISM, AND ROMANCE

1.  Lawrence W. Jones, *John Steinbeck as Fabulist*, ed. M. LaFrance (*SMS*, No. 3, 1973), pp. 18, 9–20, 3–34, provides a brilliant study of the topic. I am indebted.

2.  Peter Lisca, *The Wide World of John Steinbeck* (New Brunswick, N.J., 1958), p. 218.

3.  Elaine Steinbeck and Robert Wallsten, *Steinbeck: A Life in Letters* (New York, 1975), p. 284.

4.  Lisca, *The Wide World*, p. 231–2.

5.  Joseph Fontenrose, *John Steinbeck: An Introduction and Interpretation* (New York, 1963), pp. 109–10.

6.  Lisca, *The Wide World*, p. 233, groups the characters as "damned, those in purgatory, and the saved or elect."

7.  Ibid., pp. 261–63.

8.  Howard Levant, *The Novels of John Steinbeck: A Critical Study* (Columbia, Mo., 1974), p. 234, quotes this passage.

9.  Steinbeck and Wallsten, *Steinbeck: A Life in Letters*, p. 303.

10. While working on the *East of Eden* manuscript in 1951, Steinbeck kept a daily record of progress through letters addressed to Pascal Covici, his editor. Published posthumously, *Journal of a Novel: The East of Eden Letters* (New York, 1969), provides a unique record of Steinbeck's opinions of the book, its problems, triumphs, and other related and unrelated matters.

11. Lester Jay Marks, *Thematic Design in the Novels of John Steinbeck* (The Hague, 1969), p. 114. Jones, *John Steinbeck as Fabulist*, p. 25.

12. Northrop Frye, *Anatomy of Criticism* (Princeton, N.J., 1957), pp. 304–5.

13. See Fontenrose, *John Steinbeck*, p. 123, for an explana-
    tion of Steinbeck's misreading of the verb "tinshol";
    Steinbeck uses "timshel," an incorrect form. The verb
    cannot be translated as "thou mayest."
14. See, for example, Levant, *The Novels*, pp. 246–8.

## 7.  SEARCHES IN THE LAST YEARS

1. Roy S. Simmonds, a review: "John Steinbeck, *The Acts
   of King Arthur and His Noble Knights*," *Steinbeck
   Quarterly* 10 (Spring, 1977), 53. Elaine Steinbeck and
   Robert Wallsten, eds., *Steinbeck: A Life in Letters*
   (New York, 1975), contains letters and biographical
   passages giving some idea of the ups and downs of
   Steinbeck's work on the manuscript. See, for example,
   pp. 540, 541, 552–54, 574–79, 821.
2. Simmonds, "Steinbeck's *The Acts*," pp. 52–57, is informative.
3. Ibid., p. 53.
4. Steinbeck and Wallsten, *Steinbeck: A Life in Letters*,
   pp. 651–3.
5. Twice in the novel, Hawley repeats the lines, "Now is
   the winter of our discontent/Made glorious summer
   by this sun of York." The original lines appear in
   Shakespeare's *The Tragedy of Richard the Third*, I,
   i, 1–8.
6. Richard Astro, "Travels with Steinbeck: The Laws of
   Thought and the Laws of Things," *Steinbeck Quarterly*
   8 (Spring, 1975), 44, 35–44.

## 8.  A CONCLUSION

1. Joseph Fontenrose, *John Steinbeck: An Introduction
   and Interpretation* (New York, 1963), pp. 139–41.
2. Horst Frenz, ed., *Nobel Lectures, Literature, 1901–
   1967*, "Acceptance" (New York, 1969), pp. 575–77.

# Bibliography

*Cup of Gold.* New York: Robert M. McBride & Co., 1929.

*The Pastures of Heaven.* New York: Brewer, Warren & Putnam, 1932.

*To a God Unknown.* New York: Robert O. Ballou, 1933.

*Tortilla Flat.* New York: Covici-Friede, 1935.

*In Dubious Battle.* New York: Covici-Friede, 1936.

"Dubious Battle in California." *The Nation,* 12 September 1936, pp. 302–4.

*Of Mice and Men.* New York: Covici-Friede, 1937.

*Of Mice and Men: A Play in Three Acts.* New York: Covici-Friede, 1937.

*The Long Valley.* New York: The Viking Press, 1938.

"Their Blood Is Strong" (pamphlet). San Francisco: Simon J. Lubin Society of California, Inc., 1938.

*The Grapes of Wrath.* New York: The Viking Press, 1939.

*The Forgotten Village.* New York: The Viking Press, 1941.

*Sea of Cortez: A Leisurely Journal of Travel and Research* (with Edward F. Ricketts). New York: The Viking Press, 1941.

*The Moon Is Down.* New York: The Viking Press, 1942.

*The Moon Is Down: A Play in Two Parts.* New York: Dramatists Play Service, Inc., 1942.

*Bombs Away: The Story of a Bomber Team.* New York: The Viking Press, 1942.

*The Red Pony.* New York: The Viking Press, 1945.

*Cannery Row.* New York: The Viking Press, 1945.

*A Medal for Benny.* Story by John Steinbeck and Jack Wagner, screenplay by Frank Butler, in *Best Film Plays—1945,* ed. John Gassner and Dudley Nichols. New York: Crown, 1946.

*The Pearl.* New York: The Viking Press, 1947.

*The Wayward Bus.* New York: The Viking Press, 1947.

*A Russian Journal* (with photographs by Robert Capa). New York: The Viking Press, 1948.

*Burning Bright.* New York: The Viking Press, 1950.

"Critics, Critics, Burning Bright." *Saturday Review of Literature,* 11 November 1950, pp. 20–21.

*The Log from the Sea of Cortez.* New York: The Viking Press, 1951.

*Viva Zapata!* Screenplay abridged in *Argosy,* February 1952.

*East of Eden.* New York: The Viking Press, 1952.

*Short Novels of John Steinbeck.* New York: The Viking Press, 1953.

*Sweet Thursday.* New York: The Viking Press, 1954.

"How to Tell Good Guys from Bad Guys." *The Reporter,* 10 March 1955, pp. 42–44.

*Pipe Dream* (musical comedy by Rodgers and Hammerstein based on *Sweet Thursday*). New York: The Viking Press, 1956.

*The Short Reign of Pippin IV: A Fabrication.* New York: The Viking Press, 1957.

*Once There Was a War.* New York: The Viking Press, 1958.

*The Winter of Our Discontent.* New York: The Viking Press, 1961.

*Travels with Charley in Search of America.* New York: Curtis Publishing Co., 1962.

*America and Americans.* New York: The Viking Press, 1966.

*Journal of a Novel: The East of Eden Letters.* New York: The Viking Press, 1969.

*The Acts of King Arthur and His Noble Knights: From the Winchester Mss. of Thomas Malory and Other Sources.* Ed. Chase Horton. New York: Farrar, Straus & Giroux, 1976.

## Works about John Steinbeck

Aaron, Daniel. *Writers on the Left*. New York, 1961.

Alexander, Stanley. "The Conflict of Form in *Tortilla Flat*." *American Literature* 40 (1968), 58–60.

Astro, Richard. *John Steinbeck and Edward F. Ricketts: The Shaping of a Novelist*. Minneapolis: University of Minnesota Press, 1973.

————. "John Steinbeck: A Biographical Portrait." In *John Steinbeck: A Dictionary of His Fictional Characters*, ed. T. Hayashi, pp. 1–24. Metuchen, N.J.: The Scarecrow Press, 1976.

————. "Steinbeck's *Sea of Cortez*." In *A Study Guide to Steinbeck: A Handbook to his Major Works*, ed. T. Hayashi, pp. 168–86. Metuchen, N.J.: Scarecrow Press, 1974.

————. "Travels with Steinbeck: The Laws of Thought and the Law of Things." *Steinbeck Quarterly* 8 (1975), 35–44.

Benson, Jackson J. "Environment as Meaning: John Steinbeck and the Great Central Valley." *Steinbeck Quarterly* 10 (1977), 12–20.

————. " 'To Tom, Who Lived It': John Steinbeck and the Man from Weedpatch." *Journal of Modern Literature* 5 (1976), 151–94.

Bracher, Fredrick. "Steinbeck and the Biological View of Man." In *Steinbeck and His Critics: A Record of Twenty-Five Years*, ed. E. W. Tedlock, Jr. and C. V. Wicker, pp. 183–96. Albuquerque: University of New Mexico Press, 1957.

Carlson, Eric W. "Symbolism in *The Grapes of Wrath*." *College English* 19 (1958), 172–75.

Carpenter, F. I. "John Steinbeck: The Philosophical Joads." *College English* 2 (1941), 315–25.

Champney, Freeman. "John Steinbeck, Californian." In *Steinbeck and His Critics: A Record of Twenty-Five Years*, ed. E. W. Tedlock, Jr., and C. V. Wicker, p. 138. Albuquerque: University of New Mexico Press, 1957.

Cox, Martha Heasley. "In Search of John Steinbeck: His People and His Land." *San Jose Studies* 1 (1975), 41–60.

Crockett, H. Kelly. "The Bible and *The Grapes of Wrath*." *College English* 24 (1962), 193–98.

DeMott, Robert. "Steinbeck's *To a God Unknown*." In *A Study Guide to Steinbeck: A Handbook to His Major Works*, ed. T. Hayashi, pp. 187–213. Metuchen, N.J., The Scarecrow Press, 1974.

Ditsky, John. "Steinbeck's 'Flight': The Ambiguity of Manhood." *Steinbeck Quarterly* 5 (1972), 80–85.

———. "Steinbeck's *Travels with Charley*: The Quest that Failed." *Steinbeck Quarterly* 8 (1975), 45–50.

Eisinger, Chester E. "Jeffersonian Agrarianism in *The Grapes of Wrath*." *University of Kansas City Review* 14 (1947), 149–54.

Fontenrose, Joseph. *John Steinbeck: An Introduction and Interpretation*. New York: Holt, Rinehart & Winston, 1963.

French, Warren, ed. *A Companion to "The Grapes of Wrath."* New York: The Viking Press, 1963.

———. *John Steinbeck*. New York: Twayne, 1961.

———. *John Steinbeck*. rev. ed. Boston: Twayne, 1975.

Frenz, Horst, ed. *Nobel Lectures, Literature, 1901–1967*. New York, 1969.

Frye, Northrop. *Anatomy of Criticism*. Princeton, N.J.: Princeton University Press, 1957.

Harkness, Bruce. "Imitation and Theme." *The Journal of Art and Aesthetic Criticism* 12 (1954), 499–500.

Hayashi, Tetsumaro, ed. *A Study Guide to Steinbeck: A Handbook to His Major Works*. Metuchen, N.J.: The Scarecrow Press, 1974.

———, ed. *John Steinbeck: A Dictionary of His Fictional Characters*. Metuchen, N.J.: The Scarecrow Press, 1976.

———, ed. *Steinbeck's Literary Dimensions: A Guide to Comparative Studies*. Metuchen, N.J.: The Scarecrow Press, 1973.

———, ed. *Steinbeck's Women: Essays in Criticism*. (Steinbeck Monograph Series, No. 9), Muncie, Ind., 1979.

Jones, Lawrence W. *John Steinbeck as Fabulist*. Ed. Marston LaFrance (Steinbeck Monograph Series, No. 3), Muncie, Ind., 1973.

————. "Poison in the Cream Puff: The Human Condition in *Cannery Row*." Ed. Marston LaFrance. *Steinbeck Society* 7 (1974), 35–40.

Levant, Howard. *The Novels of John Steinbeck: A Critical Study*. Columbia: University of Missouri Press, 1974.

Lisca, Peter. "The Dynamics of Community in *The Grapes of Wrath*." In *From Irving to Steinbeck: Studies of American Literature in Honor of Harry R. Warfel*, ed. M. Deakin and P. Lisca, pp. 124–25. Gainesville, Fla., 1972.

————, ed. *The Grapes of Wrath: Text and Criticism*. New York: The Viking Press, 1972.

————. "John Steinbeck: A Literary Biography." In *Steinbeck and His Critics: A Record of Twenty-Five Years*, ed. E. W. Tedlock, Jr., and C. V. Wicker, pp. 3–22. Albuquerque: University of New Mexico Press, 1957.

————. *The Wide World of John Steinbeck*. New Brunswick, N.J.: Rutgers University Press, 1958.

McCarthy, Paul. "House and Shelter as Symbol in *The Grapes of Wrath*." *South Dakota Review* 5 (Winter 1967–68), 48–67.

Marks, Lester Jay. *Thematic Design in The Novels of John Steinbeck*. The Hague: Mouten, 1969.

Moore, Harry T. *The Novels of John Steinbeck: A First Critical Study*. Chicago: Normandie House, 1939. 2nd ed. New York: Kennikat Press, 1968.

Peterson, Richard. "The Turning Point: *The Pastures of Heaven*." In *A Study Guide to Steinbeck: A Handbook to His Major Works*, ed. T. Hayashi, pp. 87–106. Metuchen, N.J.: The Scarecrow Press, 1974.

Rideout, Walter B. *The Radical Novel in the United States, 1900–1954: Some Interrelations of Literature and Society*. Cambridge, Mass.: Harvard University Press, 1956.

Ross, Woodburn O. "John Steinbeck: Earth and Stars." In *Steinbeck and His Critics: A Record of Twenty-Five Years*, ed. E. W. Tedlock, Jr., and C. V. Wicker, pp. 167–82. Albuquerque: University of New Mexico Press, 1957.

Shockley, Martin S. "Christian Symbolism in *The Grapes of Wrath*." *College English* 18 (1956), 87–90.

————. "The Reception of *The Grapes of Wrath* in Oklahoma." In *A Companion to The Grapes of Wrath*, ed. Warren French, pp. 117–29. New York: The Viking Press, 1963.

Simmonds, Roy S. A review: "John Steinbeck, *The Acts of King Arthur and His Noble Knights*." *Steinbeck Quarterly* 10 (1977), 52–57.

Steinbeck, Elaine, and Robert Wallsten, eds. *Steinbeck: A Life in Letters*. New York: The Viking Press, 1975.

Tedlock, E. W., Jr., and C. V. Wicker, eds. *Steinbeck and His Critics: A Record of Twenty-Five Years*. Albuquerque: University of New Mexico Press, 1957.

Valjean, Nelson. *John Steinbeck, The Errant Knight: An Intimate Biography of His California Years*. San Francisco: Chronicle Books, 1975.

Watt, F. W. *John Steinbeck*. New York: Grove Press, 1962.

# Index